Improve your Skills

Reading *for IELTS*

with Answer Key

4.5–6.0

Sam McCarter • Norman Whitby

MACMILLAN

Macmillan Education
4 Crinan Street London N1 9XW
A division of Macmillan Publishers Limited
Companies and representatives throughout the world

ISBN 978-0-2304-6214-4 (with key)
ISBN 978-0-2304-6220-5 (without key)
ISBN 978-0-230-4-6217-5 (with key + MPO pack)
ISBN 978-0-230-4-6219-9 (without key + MPO pack)

Designed by Kamae Design, Oxford

Illustrated by Kamae Design, p8, 15, 22, 28, 64. Ed McLachlan, p32.

Cover photograph by Getty Images/Nick Daly
Picture research by Susannah Jayes

Sam McCarter and Norman Whitby would like to thank the editors.

The publishers would like to thank all those who participated in the development of
the project, with special thanks to the freelance editors.

The authors and publishers would like to thank the following for permission to
reproduce their photographs:
Alamy/Susan E. Degginger p27, Alamy/Ray Roberts p38, Alamy/Tony West p78(cl), Ala-
my/Rob Whitworth p22(tl); **Bananastock** pp43,78(cm); **Corbis**/Kidstock/Blend Images
p36, Corbis/Keith Levit/*/Design Pics p75, Corbis/Peter M. Fisher p54(bl), Corbis/Hero
Images/Hero Images p55, Corbis/Egmont Strigl/imagebroker p6, Corbis/moodboard
p59(tr), Corbis/Nicolas Tibaut/Photononstop p7, Corbis/VStock LLC/Klaus Tiedge/Tetra
Images p59(cr); **DigitalStock**/Corbis p14(cm); **Getty Images** p63, Getty Images/zhang
bo p54(cl), Getty Images/Austin Bush p78(cr), Getty Images/Robert Churchill p46(cr),
Getty Images/Sam Edwards p40, Getty Images/Jose Luis Pelaez Inc p30(cr), Getty Im-
ages/Stock4B p22(cl), Getty Images/Brent Winebrenner p48; **MACMILLAN NEW ZEA-
LAND** p22(bl); **Macmillan Publishers Ltd** p15(cl); **PHOTODISC** p67; **Photoshot**/
EFE p46(cl), Photoshot/NHPA p11; **José V. Resino** p52; **Superstock**/Blend Images p71,
Superstock/Corbis p30(cl), Superstock/Photononstop p80, Superstock/Tips Images p54
(bcl); **Thinkstock**/Istockphoto pp15,70.

Contents

Introduction

What is *Improve your IELTS Reading Skills*?

Improve your IELTS Reading Skills is a complete preparation course for students at score bands 4.5–6.00 preparing for the Academic Reading component of the International English Language Testing System (IELTS). Through targeted practice, it develops skills and language to help you achieve a higher IELTS score in the Academic Reading component. The course can be used with *Improve your IELTS Writing Skills* and *Improve your IELTS Listening & Speaking Skills*.

How can I use *Improve your IELTS Reading Skills*?

You can use *Improve your IELTS Reading Skills* as a book for studying on your own or in a class.

If you are studying on your own, *Improve your IELTS Reading Skills* is designed to guide you step by step through the activities. The book is also completely self-contained: a clear and accessible key is provided, so you can easily check your answers as you work through the book.

If you are studying as part of a class, your teacher will direct you on how to use each activity. Some activities can be treated as discussions, in which case they can be a useful opportunity to share ideas and techniques with other learners.

How is *Improve your IELTS Reading Skills* organized?

It consists of ten units based around topics which occur commonly in the real test.

Each unit consists of three sections:

Skills: exercises and examples to develop reading skills and build confidence for the exam.

The skills section is subdivided further into sections. These focus on specific types of questions that occur in the exam.

Word skills for IELTS: practice of useful vocabulary for the Academic Reading.

Reading Passage: a practice test with questions to develop skills for reading.

In addition, there are Technique boxes throughout the book. These reinforce key points on how to approach Academic Reading tasks.

How will *Improve your IELTS Reading Skills* improve my score?

By developing skills

The skills sections form a detailed syllabus of essential IELTS reading skills. The full range of question types is covered. For example, key IELTS tasks like *Matching headings* and dealing with *True/False/Not Given* statements are dealt with clearly and then practised in a reading test.

By developing language

Each unit also contains a resource of useful phrases and vocabulary to use in each reading test. Over the course of *Improve your IELTS Reading Skills*, you will encounter a wide range of ideas to ensure that you are well prepared when you reach the real test. These include concepts such as recognizing general nouns, recognizing organization, analysing questions and understanding meaning to increase your speed so that you can approach the Academic Reading component with confidence.

By developing test technique

The Technique boxes contain procedures which can easily be memorized and used as reminders in the real test. These include quick and easy advice about how to tackle particular types of questions and how to use the skills you have learned effectively.

How is the IELTS Academic Reading component organized?

The Academic Reading component of the IELTS lasts one hour. In the test, there are three reading passages of different lengths and increasing difficulty with 40 questions.

What does each task consist of?

The passages are taken from a range of sources: books, magazines, newspapers and journals. At least one of the articles contains a detailed argument. The range of questions used in the exam are as follows:

- multiple-choice questions
- short answer questions
- sentence completion
- notes, flow chart, table completion
- labelling a diagram/map
- summary completion with and without wordlists
- classification
- matching information to paragraphs
- matching paragraph/section headings
- identification of information – True/False/Not Given
- identification of writer's views/claims – Yes/No/Not Given

In the exam, you will probably only have a selection of the above types of question, but you need to be familiar with all of them.

How will I be assessed?

The Academic Reading component is weighted. This means that the standard for each exam is the same, but the number of correct answers required to achieve that standard will vary from exam to exam. For example, in order to achieve a score band 7, you should aim to have a minimum of 29 or 30 correct answers.

Therefore, keep in mind that as you do different reading passages in the book, the number of correct answers in each will probably be different. This reflects the nature of the IELTS exam as some passages may appear to be easier or more difficult than others.

If you are aiming for a score band 7, for example, we would expect you to answer approximately 9 or 10 correctly from each passage over three passages. In the real test, this is equal to 29 or 30 over three passages, but remember that in exam conditions your performance may not be the same.

How much time should I spend on each reading passage?

It is advisable to spend twenty minutes on each reading passage and to write your answers directly onto the answer sheet. You do not have time at the end to transfer your answers from the test booklet.

If you cannot answer a question quickly, leave it and move on to the next question. Then come back to it if you can. As a rough guide, you will have a maximum of one and a half minutes to answer each question.

Since the passages become progressively more difficult, do each passage in order.

Note that your spelling in the answers needs to be correct.

1 Change
and consequences

UNIT AIMS

READING SKILLS
Scanning
Completing sentences (gapped)
Answering True/False/Not Given
statements

EXAM PRACTICE
Answering True/False/Not Given
statements
Completing sentences (gapped)
Completing multiple-choice questions

Scanning

1 Look at the photo and answer the
questions below.

  a What are the main causes of the
    expanding desert in the picture?
  b Do you think the situation can be
    reversed? If so, what can be done?
  c Is the responsibility for trying to stop
    this problem local or global?
  d What are the consequences to
    mankind in general? Are they social,
    economic or environmental?

2 Look quickly at the block of text. Find the words *Sahel* and *desertification*
and underline them. Then answer the questions below.

> dkdnnvtruenncmcompletinomnSahelvocmdessertnfindf
> ksssjoodesertificationdeesosjdvfnvffkmvmdmvfalsekdw
> rfvdcnvtextadnvmlfflkjvirhgijflvnlkokdfnkfkfvflkdvkkjn

  a Why can you see the word *Sahel* easily? Choose a reason.
    because it is a large word
    because it is in the middle of the text
    because it has a capital letter
    because you don't have to look for the meaning.
  b Can you see the word *desertification* as easily? Why/Why not?

Technique
Scan any text or image to
find a word or phrase. Do
not aim to understand the
whole text. Aim only to
find the word or phrase.

3 Decide which suggestions a–g are most helpful for scanning. Add your own
suggestions.

  a Look only for specific words or phrases.
  b Look for each word or phrase in turn.
  c Look at every word in the text.
  d Try not to think of the meaning as you scan.
  e Use a pencil to guide you.
  f Underline the word when you find it.
  g Think of the meaning of the word you are looking for.

4 Scan the text to find the words below and underline them. The first word has been underlined for you.

zone ■ marginal ■ steadily crept ■ Botswana ■ increasing population ■ overcultivation plant species ■ management

DEFORESTATION AND DESERTIFICATION

A The Sahel <u>zone</u> lies between the Sahara desert and the fertile savannahs of northern Nigeria and southern Sudan. The word *sahel* comes from Arabic and means marginal or transitional, and this
5 is a good description of these semi-arid lands, which occupy much of the West African countries of Mali, Mauritania, Niger and Chad.

10 **B** Unfortunately, over the last century the Sahara desert has steadily crept southwards, eating into once productive Sahel lands. United Nations surveys show that over 70 per cent of the dry land in agricultural use in Africa has deteriorated over the last 30 years. Droughts have become more prolonged and more severe, the most recent lasting over 20 years in parts of the Sahel region. The same process of desertification
15 is taking place across southern Africa as the Kalahari desert advances into Botswana and parts of South Africa.

C One of the major causes of this desert advance is poor agricultural land use, driven by the pressures of increasing population. Overgrazing – keeping too many farm animals on the land – means that grasses and other plants cannot recover, and scarce water
20 supplies are exhausted. Overcultivation – trying to grow too many crops on poor land – results in the soil becoming even less fertile and drier, and beginning to break up. Soil erosion follows, and the land turns into desert.

D Another cause of desertification is loss of tree cover. Trees are cut down for use as fuel and to clear land for agricultural use. Tree roots help to bind the soil together, to
25 conserve moisture and to provide a habitat for other plants and animals. When trees are cut down, the soil begins to dry and loosen, wind and rain erosion increase, other plant species die and eventually the fertile topsoil may be almost entirely lost, leaving only bare rock and dust.

E The effects of loss of topsoil and increased drought are irreversible. They are,
30 however, preventable. Careful conservation of tree cover and sustainable agricultural land use have been shown to halt deterioration of soils and lessen the effects of shortage of rainfall. One project in Kita in south-west Mali funded by the UNDP has involved local communities in sustainable management of forest, while at the same time providing a viable agricultural economy based on the production of soaps,
35 beekeeping and marketing shea nuts. This may be a model for similar projects in other West African countries.

5 When you scan for a word or phrase, avoid looking at other words. Diagrams 1–5 show five techniques for doing this. Match each diagram with the correct description a–e.

  a Scan the text in a zigzag from right to left. Look at either side of the zigzag line.

  b Scan from the bottom right to left, then left to right.

  c Scan from the bottom. Move right to left, right to left.

  d Scan vertically from the bottom to the top. Look at either side of the line.

  e Scan from the bottom right of a paragraph to the top left. Look at either side of the diagonal line.

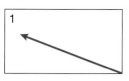

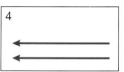

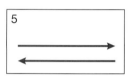

6 Use the scanning technique in diagram 4, exercise 5 to find the following words in the *Deforestation and Desertification* passage. Then underline them.

> transitional ▪ unfortunately ▪ surveys ▪ severe ▪ exhausted ▪ bind
> eventually ▪ shea

7 Use the scanning technique in diagram 2, exercise 5 to find words and phrases with these meanings. Use the paragraph reference and the first letter to help you.

  a It begins with *o* and means *cover*. (Paragraph A)

  b It begins with *t* and means *happening*. (Paragraph B)

  c It begins with *s* and means *limited*. (Paragraph C)

  d It begins with *e* and means *completely*. (Paragraph D)

  e It begins with *h* and means *stop*. (Paragraph E)

8 Choose a scanning technique from the options given in exercise 5. Scan the whole text for words or phrases with these meanings. The words are not necessarily in the order of the text.

  a It begins with *p* and means *long*.

  b It begins with *p* and means *fertile*.

  c It begins with *e* and means *wearing away*.

9 Build up a revision list of scanning techniques on a card or in your notebook.

Technique

Keep revision cards of reading techniques such as those for scanning. Remember to use and try a range of techniques for all reading skills and not just one.

Completing sentences (gapped)

1 Read sentences 1–6 taken from a Sentence completion task. Decide whether the missing words are adjectives or nouns/noun phrases.

> **1** The climate of the Sahel is described as _____ .
>
> **2** In some areas of the Sahel, there has been no rainfall for more than
>
> _____ .
>
> **3** Desertification is caused by overgrazing, but this in turn is due to the pressure from _____ .
>
> **4** When trees are cut down, the soil is affected, which leads to the death of the surrounding _____ .
>
> **5** The consequences of the loss of topsoil cannot be reversed, but they are
>
> _____ .
>
> **6** Looking after trees reduces the consequences of a lack of
>
> _____ .

Technique

Look out for the answers to the Gapped sentence completion in the text. New and important information is often at the end or towards the end of the sentence. Notice where answers to questions are in the reading passage, e.g. questions 2 and 3. This will help your scanning and prediction techniques.

2 Scan the reading passage on the previous page using one of the techniques in exercise 5 and complete the sentences in exercise 1. Choose NO MORE THAN TWO WORDS from the passage for each answer.

Answering True/False/Not Given statements

1 Statements 1–7 in exercise 2 are taken from a True/False/Not Given task. Underline words which could be used to scan the passage. Explain your choices.

Example
The semi-arid land of the Sahel is found only in <u>Mali</u>.
Scan for Mali because it is easy to see (capital letter) and cannot be expressed in another way.

2 Look again at the statements in 1–7 below. Underline words that qualify or limit each statement, especially adverbs and adjectives.

Example
The semi-arid land of the Sahel is found <u>only</u> in Mali.

> **1** The Sahara has spread slowly northwards into the Sahel region.
>
> **2** Just over 70 per cent of the dry land in agricultural use in Africa has deteriorated over the last 30 years.
>
> **3** Desertification is taking place faster in southern Africa than in the Sahel.
>
> **4** The advance of the desert is not the result of poor agricultural land use.
>
> **5** The loss of tree cover is a minor cause of desertification.
>
> **6** If there is a loss of tree cover, the deterioration in the soil is halted.
>
> **7** Tree conservation is more effective than sustainable agricultural land use in reducing the consequences of lack of rain.

3 Decide whether the statements in exercise 2 are False or Not Given according to the passage.

4 Explain why each statement 1–4 below is Not Given in the text. Use the example to help you.

Example
The Sahel covers more of the land in Mali than it does in Chad.
Not Given because there is no comparison in the text. We know that it covers much of Mali and Chad, but we do not know which country has more.

> **1** Agricultural land in Africa could deteriorate further in the coming years.
>
> **2** There could be another severe drought in the Sahel over the next three decades.
>
> **3** In some areas, the UNDP may provide financial support for forestry management to local communities in the future.
>
> **4** A second project has been planned in Mali to develop sustainable forestry management.

Technique

Keep a list of the common grammatical structures you come across in *True/False/Not Given* sentences with examples, e.g. comparison and contrast (The Sahel covers more of the land in Mali than it does in Chad), cause and effect, present simple for general statements, time phrases.

Improve your IELTS word skills

1 Identify the type of words in the box below. Are they (a) general nouns which need a context for their meaning or (b) nouns which have specific meaning?

consequence ▪ factor ▪ change ▪ result ▪ impact ▪ effect ▪ cause ▪ role

2 Complete the sentences with a word from the box above. Some will need to be put in the plural form.

a Technology has had a huge _____ on our lives.

b The area has undergone many _____ in recent years.

c Planting trees can have a knock-on _____ on the economy of arid areas.

d Deforestation can have unforeseen _____ for the ecology of a region.

e It is sometimes difficult to discover the exact _____ of a problem.

f To achieve the best _____, it is important to initiate change at a local level.

g The main _____ contributing to success in any organization is a happy workforce.

h The climate has played a major _____ in this region's economic history.

> **Technique**
> Make a list of general nouns like the ones in the box above. Write a phrase to go with each one to put it in context. General nouns are useful in all parts of the exam.

3 Complete the sentences with a phrase from the box.

gradual development ▪ limited impact ▪ far-reaching consequences
dramatic changes ▪ favourable outcome ▪ underlying cause ▪ profound effect

a Government intervention has had _____ for regional growth.

b Shock tactics can bring about _____ in people's behaviour.

c _____ is much more acceptable than rapid change.

d The introduction of new farming practices has had a _____ on people's lives.

e To achieve the most _____ the countries involved need to negotiate.

f The _____ in this particular case is not easy to find.

g The huge sums invested had only a _____ on the neighbourhood.

> **Technique**
> Keep lists of general nouns with possible adjective collocations. Use the *Macmillan Collocations Dictionary*. This will help to build your vocabulary range for the other skills as well as reading.

4 Decide whether the words in brackets have the same or opposite meaning to the words in italics.

Example
Tourists have changed the coastline *dramatically*. (slightly) *Opposite meaning*

a The wasteland was *completely* transformed. (totally)
b The government *fully* accept the consequences of their actions. (partially)
c The marine life in the coral reef is *highly* sensitive to temperature fluctuations. (exceedingly)
d Alternative sources of energy like solar power can *vastly* improve life in remote communities. (marginally)
e The rising sea level will *greatly* affect the livelihoods of people on some Pacific islands. (considerably)

Reading Passage 1

You should spend 20 minutes on questions 1–14, which are based on Reading Passage 1 below.

Technique

Follow these stages when you look at a reading passage and the associated questions:

1 Survey the title, text and questions in three or four seconds.

2 Use the title to think of the contents of the text.

3 Skim the text and questions. You should aim to eventually do this in two minutes.

4 Use the information from the question to help you to scan and locate the answers in the reading passage.

Swallows in Migration

Every April, along with many other species of birds, the swallow arrives to spend the summer months in northern Europe, in Russia, Iran and parts of Siberia. Here it will breed and raise its young. [5]

The swallow is well known for several reasons. Firstly, it is very distinctive, with its forked tail and characteristic acrobatic swooping flight. Secondly, it is very common, and, like its near relative the house martin, lives in close proximity to human habitation, at least in rural areas. [10] It is, however, rarely to be encountered in towns or cities.

For centuries, people have observed swallows, noted their arrival and their patterns of feeding. In several countries, these observations have passed into the language as proverbs or sayings. In England, people comment on unpredictable [15] late spring weather by saying, 'one swallow does not a summer make'. Similarly, 'the swallows are flying low' was held to predict rainy, even stormy weather. There may be [20] some truth in this observation, though it is the insects the swallows feed on that seem to be more susceptible to the fall in barometric pressure that heralds a storm. Insects keep low in these conditions, and so do the swallows that hunt them. At the end of the summer season, when the swallows are about to leave, they frequently flock together in large numbers on convenient high open perches, like roof ridges and telegraph wires. When people remark that 'the swallows are gathering', they mean that autumn has arrived.

At some point in mid-September the swallows leave together, usually all on the same day. One day there are thousands, the next there are none, and none will be seen again until the following spring. For centuries, this was a complete mystery to people. The Hampshire naturalist Gilbert White, writing in the late eighteenth century, believed that the swallows dived into ponds and rivers in autumn and remained in the bottom mud the whole winter, re-emerging the following spring. This idea seems extraordinary to us, but White was not a stupid man: many of his other observations of natural life were informed and accurate. In this case, however, he simply had no means of determining the truth and was forced to make a random guess. The idea that swallows migrate to central or southern Africa would have seemed as fanciful to him as his theory seems to us.

Although we now know that swallows migrate, there are still unanswered questions. Why do they go so far? Why not stay on the shores of the Mediterranean? The majority continue to equatorial Africa, and some even further south. Also it appears that populations of swallows that have bred in different countries also spend the winter in different areas. Those from France, Germany and much of western Europe have mostly been traced to East Africa, Kenya or Tanzania for example. Above all, how does a bird weighing approximately twenty grams find its way across mountain ranges, ocean and desert to winter in the south, and then return the following year to the very location it was born, in some cases to the very same nest?

Birds can navigate by the Sun, and are also able to detect the magnetic field of the Earth. Species that migrate at night are also able to navigate by the stars. By these means, they travel long distances. The close navigation that brings them back to the same field or nest appears to be related to memory of local landmarks imprinted on the minds of young birds as they crisscross the area in the weeks before departure.

Nevertheless, the journey is very dangerous. Long sea crossings, where there is little available food or water, are generally avoided. In western Europe, most swallows cross to Africa via the Straits of Gibraltar, or fly the length of Italy before tackling the relatively short crossing to Tunisia in North Africa. However, in storms they may be blown hundreds of kilometres off course. Exhausted swallows sometimes come to rest on ships way out in the Atlantic Ocean. They have to cross mountain ranges too, where again the weather may be unpredictable and food scarce. Along the coast of North Africa, many young swallows become the prey of Eleonora's falcons, which time their breeding to coincide with the migration of young birds southwards. But the most dangerous part of the journey is the crossing of the Sahara desert. Here, there is little food or water, sandstorms may delay and exhaust the already weakened birds, and many die. It is estimated that around 50 per cent of adult birds die, and up to 80 per cent of young birds, but enough survive to ensure the continuation of the species.

Questions 1–6

Do the following statements agree with the information given in the passage?

Write

> **TRUE**   *if the statement agrees with the information*
> **FALSE**   *if the statement contradicts the information*
> **NOT GIVEN**   *if there is no information on this*

1   The swallow is the only species of bird that migrates to spend the summer in northern Europe.

2   The swallow is easily noticeable because of its tail and the way it flies.

3   The swallow is frequently seen in cities.

4   The insects, not the swallows themselves, appear to predict stormy weather.

5   Swallows form larger flocks than other birds when they depart in the autumn.

6   White's theory seems strange to people now.

Questions 7–12

Complete the sentences.

*Choose **NO MORE THAN TWO WORDS** from the passage for each answer.*

7   In the past, the destination of the swallows in autumn was a ....

8   As White could not verify what happened to the swallows, he made a ....

9   Despite knowing that swallows migrate, we are still left with ....

10 Sometimes, swallows have been known to return not just to the same area, but even to the ....

11 Birds that travel by night can find their way using the ....

12 Bird navigation appears to be connected with the memory of ....

Questions 13 and 14

*Choose **TWO** letters, **A–F**.*

Which **TWO** of the following dangers faced by swallows during migration are mentioned in the text?

A   The Sahara desert   D   Hungry sailors

B   Long sea crossings   E   Eleonora's falcons

C   Lack of nesting places   F   The crossing to Tunisia

Technique

True/False/Not Given

1 Look for words in each statement to help you scan.

2 Identify comparisons or qualifying expressions in the statements.

3 Try to predict some answers.

4 Find your scan words in the text then read around them closely to locate the answers. Remember that the answers follow the order of the reading passage.

Technique

Sentence completion

1 Remember that the answers follow the order of the passage.

2 Note the word limit for each gap.

3 Look for words in each sentence to help you scan.

4 Find your scan words in the text. Think of the part of the sentence the answer might be in: the beginning or the end. Then read around them to locate the answers. Note in the sentences for completion: 'a' before the gap = singular countable noun, no article = plural or uncountable noun, the = any noun.

Skimming

1 Look at the photos and answer questions a–d below.

a Where are the places shown in the photos? Can you think of other famous historical monuments around the world?

b Are places like these relevant in any way to the modern world? How?

c Do you think knowing the past helps us to define the future? Or do you think studying history is not important?

d Is there a historical place in your home country which is special to you?

2 Which alternative (a–d) below best explains how to skim?

a You extract the meaning or topic of a text without looking at all of the words.

b You read every word as fast as you can.

c You look for one word or phrase only.

d You look at a text in detail.

3 Read the lists of words 1–5 and answer questions a–d.

1 architect building skyscraper construct design

2 train travel passenger ticket luggage

3 nostalgia past memories read former times history

4 airport luggage air steward fly aeroplane boarding pass

5 in the up to the of a of the enormous and that we with the in

a Which list is connected with the topic of air travel?

b Which list refers to no clear topic?

c What do you think is the topic of each of the other three?

d What types of words are in lists 1–4? How is 5 different?

Technique

Learn to skim reading passages quickly. In the exam you should skim the reading passage in two minutes or less and then skim the questions. Remember in the IELTS exam you are not meant to study all the text in detail, but to understand and extract information quickly, so you need to learn to skim quickly.

4 Read the title of the passage below. Underline the words in the box which you would expect to see in the passage. How do the words relate to the title?

football ▪ construction ▪ bridges ▪ hairdressing ▪ engineers ▪ dictionary ▪ industrial ▪ projects ▪ railway

The greatest of Victorian engineers

A In the hundred years up to 1860, the work of a small group of construction engineers carried forward the enormous social and economic change that we associate with the Industrial Revolution in Britain. The most important of these engineers was Isambard Kingdom
5 Brunel, whose work in shipping, bridge-building and railway construction, to name just three fields, both challenged and motivated his colleagues. He was the driving force behind a number of hugely ambitious projects, some of which resulted in works which are still in use today.

B The son of an engineer, Brunel apprenticed with his father at an early
10 age on the building of the Thames Tunnel. At the age of just twenty, he became the engineer in charge of the project. This impressive plan to bore under the Thames twice suffered major disasters when the river broke through into the tunnel. When the second breach occurred in 1827, Brunel was seriously injured during rescue operations and further work was halted.

C While recovering from his injuries, Brunel entered a design competition for a new bridge over the
15 Avon Gorge near Clifton, Bristol. The original judge of the competition was Thomas Telford, a leading civil engineer of his day, who rejected all entries to the competition in favour of his own design. After considerable scandal, a second contest was held and Brunel's design was accepted. For reasons of funding, however, exacerbated by social unrest in Bristol, the project was abandoned in 1843 with only the towers completed. After Brunel's death, it was decided to begin work on it again, partly so that the bridge could
20 form a fitting memorial to the great engineer. Work was finally completed in 1864. Today, the well known Clifton Suspension Bridge is a symbol of Bristol, just as the Opera House is of Sydney. Originally intended only for horse-drawn traffic, the bridge now bears over four million motor vehicles a year.

5 Read the title again and skim paragraph A. Look only at the words that are connected with the word *engineer*. Ignore the other words as in the diagram. Which words would you skim?

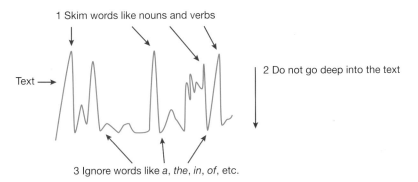

1 Skim words like nouns and verbs

Text →

2 Do not go deep into the text

3 Ignore words like *a*, *the*, *in*, *of*, etc.

Technique

Skim a reading passage using only words like nouns, noun phrases and verbs. These are the words that give you meaning. They give you the gist of the passage. You can look at the other function words like *a*, *the*, *in*, *of*, etc. when you read a passage more closely. Remember skimming is a stage in the reading process. Close reading comes later.

6 Skim the whole text in exercise 4 and match each title below with a paragraph. Which words in the text help you match the title?

1 The contest for and construction of a suspension bridge
2 An inspiring engineer
3 The construction of a tunnel under a river

Answering True/False/Not Given statements

1 Statements 1–7 are taken from a True/False/Not Given task. These often contain comparison structures. Read the statements and underline phrases which contain a comparison.

Technique

Keep in mind that True/False/Not Given statements check factual information in the reading passage.

> **1** Brunel was less important than the other construction engineers in Britain during the Industrial Revolution.
>
> **2** Brunel was less involved in railway construction than other engineering fields.
>
> **3** Brunel worked only on shipping, bridge-building and railway construction.
>
> **4** Brunel's work was largely ignored by his colleagues.
>
> **5** All projects Brunel contributed to are still used today.
>
> **6** Brunel became an apprentice with his father at the same age as other engineers.
>
> **7** The Thames Tunnel Project was more difficult than any previous construction venture undertaken in Britain.

2 Decide whether the statements in exercise 1 are False or Not Given.

3 Make simple changes to statements 1–3 in exercise 1 to make them True.

4 The flow chart below shows how to decide between True, False and Not Given in comparison statements. Complete the flow chart by inserting *True*, *False* or *Not Given* into the appropriate gaps a–c.

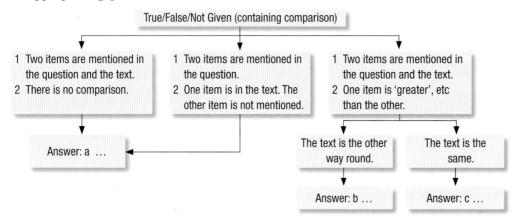

5 Look at the reading passage on page 15 and decide whether the statements below are False or Not Given. Use the flow chart in exercise 4 to help you.

Technique

Use the diagram to think about sentences containing cause and effect True/False/Not Given statements. Draw a similar diagram to show how to decide for cause and effect statements.

> **1** More change took place during the Industrial Revolution than has happened since.
>
> **2** Brunel was involved in more engineering fields than his colleagues.
>
> **3** Brunel was less influential than his colleagues in some of the works that survive today.

Completing sentences (matching endings)

1 Read the sentence beginnings 1–7. Which two beginnings are most likely to be followed by an effect?

Technique
Learn to notice and record the range of functions and grammar structures used in all types of reading questions, not just sentence completion tasks.

1 Thomas Telford

2 Scandal about the result of the first competition

3 Brunel's design for the bridge

4 Funding problems

5 The towers

6 Work on the bridge

7 The Clifton Suspension Bridge

2 Read the sentence endings A–H. Decide which endings indicate an effect. Then make questions by adding a question word to each ending.

Example
A *Which* were the only parts of the bridge completed during Brunel's lifetime.

A were the only parts of the bridge completed during Brunel's lifetime.

B was an important civil engineer.

C meant the completion of the bridge was delayed.

D is a symbol of Bristol.

E was recommenced as a suitable memorial to Brunel.

F was chosen in the second competition.

G led to a second contest to design the bridge.

H symbolizes Sydney.

3 Based on your answers in exercise 2, predict which sentence beginnings and endings can possibly match up. Then skim paragraph C in the passage and match each sentence beginning 1–7 with the correct ending A–H.

4 Read the following statements from a Sentence completion task which a student matched. Decide which statements are correct and which are wrong and recombine the sentences. Give reasons for the changes you make.

a Many historical sites worldwide are often rewritten by historians.

b Many old films are rarely conducted for a long period of time.

c Archaeological digs were known for their breadth of knowledge.

d Samuel Johnson and Leonardo da Vinci are being destroyed by visitors.

e Past events are being restored and digitally mastered.

f Past events are inaccessible to us, even more so than a distant place.

Unit 2

Improve your IELTS word skills

1 Match each precise date below with the more general period.

| 1952 ■ 1798 ■ 1891 ■ 1803 ■ 2001 ■ 1921 ■ 1854 |

   a in the early decades of the twentieth century
   b in the late nineteenth century
   c just after the turn of the nineteenth century
   d in the 1850s
   e in the mid twentieth century
   f close to the millennium
   g in the late eighteenth century

2 Scan the text on pages 19 and 20 to find four examples of general time phrases.

3 Complete each sentence a–g with the most suitable ending 1–7.
   a The committee will make every
   b On the whole, the government achieved
   c Unfortunately, he did not fulfil
   d The campaigners worked
   e The local authority drew up
   f The directors set
   g The king declared that he had no

   1 his ambition to become a historian.
   2 a scheme to restore the old mill to working order.
   3 endeavour to help those most in need.
   4 very high sales targets for the final quarter.
   5 its main aim of redistributing wealth.
   6 towards their goal for many years.
   7 intention of giving up his authority.

> ### Technique
> 1 Look at the beginnings a–g and think of possible collocations for the verbs.
> 2 Skim the endings 1–7 and match them with the beginnings.

4 In which sentences in Exercise 3 is it possible to say whether the intentions, schemes, etc were successful or not?

5 Decide whether the following words and phrases introduce an action: which came before the one in the previous section of text (B); and which introduce an action which came after (A)?

   1 Following this , _A_
   2 Previously, _____
   3 Some years earlier _____
   4 Subsequently, _____
   5 Prior to this, _____
   6 Some months later, _____
   7 This had been caused by _____
   8 The result of this was _____
   9 The response was to _____
   10 By this time, _____

Reading Passage 2

1 You should spend 20 minutes on questions 1–14 which are based on Reading Passage 2.

Technique

Survey the title, the reading passage and the questions within about 8–10 seconds to understand what your task is. Read the title and skim the text then the questions. Decide what type of passage it is: mainly historical, problem and solution or argumentative?

Chartism: a people's petition to Parliament

The early decades of the 1800s are well known as a period of discontent and social unrest. The Industrial Revolution meant the decline of traditional rural communities and the growth of a working-class urban population, particularly in the new industrial towns of the North such as Manchester. Living and working conditions for the urban factory worker were frequently
5 appalling and gave rise to a number of movements aimed at bettering working-class conditions. One such movement was Chartism, which aimed to present a people's charter, or petition for reform, to parliament. It had a number of aims, but first and foremost among them was the granting of universal suffrage, or the vote for all men over the age of 21.

There had been several previous attempts in the early 1800s to build a solid working-class
10 movement, most notably the attempt to establish a universal trade union known as the Grand National Consolidated Trade Union or GNCTU. In 1834, however, this trade union collapsed. The subsequent disillusionment led to a growth of interest in other possible ways of giving voice to the desires and grievances of the workers. In 1836, the London Working Men's Association was founded, led by William Lovett. Its aim was to reform parliament, and in 1838 it issued a charter
15 demanding six political reforms, including universal suffrage. Most of these demands were to be taken up by the Chartist petitioners.

So began the Chartist movement. Other centres of this movement were located in Birmingham, and in the north of England. In Birmingham, the movement was championed by Thomas Attwood, a banker who was interested in leading the movement for parliamentary reform in
20 the Midlands, and Joseph Sturge, a wealthy corn merchant. The key figure in the north of England was Fergus O'Connor, at that time the editor of the newspaper *The Northern Star*. In 1839, a Chartist National Convention assembled in London. The delegates talked of proclaiming a 'sacred month' or general strike, and collected signatures for a great petition. This petition was presented to parliament but it was rejected in the Commons by 235 votes to 46. Thereupon the
25 National Convention proclaimed a general strike, but a week later cancelled the proclamation and ignominiously dismissed itself. The government meanwhile had taken action and additional troops had been sent to those areas where Chartism was strongest. Disturbances in Birmingham were crushed, and William Lovett was arrested. The only other Chartist rising occurred in Monmouthshire where a group of miners marched in Newport. Again, this Newport Rising was
30 quickly crushed and its leaders transported for life.

In 1842, a second petition was presented to parliament but was again rejected by 287 votes to 49. A series of riots and strikes followed, most notably the Lancashire Plug Plot, where strikers went round the mills removing the plugs from boilers. Again, government troops moved in to crush all such disturbances and many Chartists were arrested. William Lovett subsequently abandoned the
35 cause, and Fergus O'Connor rose to prominence as the main Chartist leader.

30   In 1848, under the leadership of O'Connor, a third Chartist petition was drawn up known as the 'Monster Petition'. It was intended to be taken to parliament in a large procession, but the government took elaborate military precautions, and the procession was forbidden to cross the Thames. It was therefore taken to parliament in three cabs instead. O'Connor had claimed that the petition contained five million signatures, but in the event it was found to contain less than two million, and a great many

35   of these were false. Parliament refused to discuss it, and the Chartist movement was discredited.

Despite the fiasco of the third petition, the Chartist movement gave expression to a number of proposals which were later adopted to produce a reformed parliamentary system. Universal manhood suffrage, the abolition of the property qualification and a secret ballot all featured among the Chartists' demands and all of them were eventually granted, but the process of reform

40   was slow and was not fully achieved until the early 20th century. In essence, the demands of the Chartists were too far ahead of the times, and consequently the government took very resolute action to control and suppress their actions. Doubtless the essayist Thomas Carlyle, writing in the mid 19th century, expressed the fear of many MPs when he wrote, 'These chartisms are our French Revolution. God grant that we, with our better methods, may be able to transact it by

45   argument alone.'

Questions 1–7

*Complete each sentence with the correct ending **A–H**.*

1   The GNCTU

2   The London Working Men's Association

3   The Chartist National Convention

4   The first Chartist petition

5   The Newport Rising

6   The Lancashire Plug Plot

7   The third Chartist petition

A   was not debated in parliament.

B   was a response to the government's rejection of the 1842 Chartist petition.

C   was a failed attempt to establish a universal workers' movement.

D   was an example of the unrest following the rejection of the 1839 petition.

E   was a response to the transportation of a number of Chartist leaders.

F   made an empty threat of industrial action.

G   was rejected in parliament by a large majority.

H   anticipated many of the demands of later Chartist petitions.

Technique

Sentence completion (matching endings)

1 Look at the beginnings. Put a box around any scanning words such as names or places.

2 Skim the endings. Look for relationships like examples, or cause and effect.

3 Predict the answers by deciding what is likely to go together.

4 Eliminate endings which cannot match. Think about collocations and meaning.

5 Use the scan words to find the right part of the text and check your answers.

Questions 8–11

Look at the following statements (Questions 8–11) and the list of people in the box below.

Match each statement with the correct person A–C.

NB *You may use any letter more than once.*

8 He led the Chartist movement in the North of England.

9 He was head of the London Working Men's Association.

10 He campaigned for parliamentary reform in the Midlands.

11 He was the movement's figurehead when the third 'Monster' petition was compiled.

List of people
A William Lovett
B Thomas Attwood
C Fergus O'Connor

Questions 12–14

Do the following statements agree with the information in the reading passage?

Write

TRUE	*if the statement agrees with the information*
FALSE	*if the statement contradicts the information*
NOT GIVEN	*if there is no information on this*

12 The 1848 Chartist procession was halted due to government intervention.

13 The third Chartist petition contained more signatures than the 1842 petition.

14 All of the Chartists' demands had been granted by 1900.

2 Make a checklist of the skills that you have learnt in Units 1 and 2. Put them into a table and keep your own notes and examples for reference.

Reading Skills Checklist

Reading Skills	Notes: comments and examples
1 Surveying a reading passage	Looking at the heading, reading passage and the questions very quickly before skimming for gist

READING SKILLS
Labelling a diagram (1)
Completing tables
Completing flow charts

EXAM PRACTICE
Labelling a diagram
Completing multiple-choice questions
Completing sentences (matching endings)

Labelling a diagram (1)

1   Describe how each energy source in the photos has had an impact on human history.

2   Answer the questions a–c below.

   a   What other energy sources can you think of? How has each one had an impact on human history?
   b   Which sources do you think have a future?
   c   What types of energy have you used so far today?

3   Look at the diagram and answer questions a and b.

   a   What does the diagram show?
   b   What types of words are needed to label the diagram? Make some predictions.

4   Label the diagram using no more than TWO words from the passage below for each blank space.

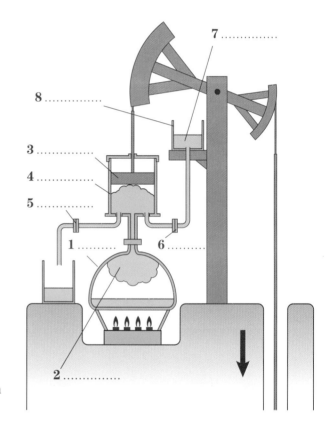

Thomas Newcomen's steam engine was one of the first devices to use the power of steam for mechanical work. It was originally used to pump water from mines. A boiler, encased in brick and sitting over a coal fire, generated steam, which drove the piston in the open top cylinder above the boiler. When the steam built up, the pressure opened a valve allowing the steam to fill the cylinder and push the piston up. When the piston reached the top of the cylinder, the first valve was closed and the second valve opened. This second valve sprayed cold water into the cylinder from a cistern, condensing the steam and creating a vacuum. The air pressure from the open-top cylinder pushed the piston down again, thus pulling the rod down with it. The cycle then repeated itself all over again.

5 Look again at the text in exercise 4. In which order does the text refer to the following?

> the source of power ∎ the use of the engine ∎ the effect of the power and following actions

6 Find and underline the following in the text.
   a an infinitive to express purpose
   b a relative clause to introduce the next action
   c a word used at the beginning of a sentence to link two actions
   d a gerund clause to refer to the effect of the previous action
   e a word meaning 'in this way' followed by a gerund.

7 Decide if the following sentences about machines are true or false. Use a dictionary to help you.
   a A washing machine contains a pump and a motor.
   b An air conditioning unit contains a coil and a fan.
   c A photocopier has various components, including rollers and a piston.
   d A filter and a tube can be found in a television.
   e A lever and a spring are component parts of a toaster.
   f A valve and a switch can be found in an aerosol spray.
   g Inside a vacuum cleaner, there is a filter and rotating brushes.

> **Technique**
> Keep a record of the various components of machines and devices and update your list regularly. Also record the purpose of the machine or device.

8 Match these verbs to the machines in exercise 6: *spray, wash, blow, vacuum, rotate, clean, cool, copy, show, toast*. Then describe the purpose of each machine using the verbs: it is used to …

9 Name one device or machine for each of the following components. Decide what the purpose of the component is in each case.

> battery ∎ axle ∎ blade ∎ handle ∎ lens ∎ turbine ∎ switch

10 Think of a device or machine, e.g. a wind turbine, a mobile phone or a tablet, and describe briefly how it works and what the purpose of the various components is.

Completing tables

1 Before you look at the passage below, decide which of the following words are associated with advantage and which with disadvantage.

> downside ∎ benefit ∎ drawback ∎ stumbling block ∎ problem ∎ upside ∎ plus ∎ handicap

The future of energy sources

A The future for petroleum use at the moment looks rather uncertain, despite enjoying the major benefit of a very advanced infrastructure already in place. The downsides from the environmental point of view are patently obvious: harm to public health through carbon dioxide emissions in exhaust fumes.

B The picture for natural gas is similarly mixed. While its main strength lies in it's being a relatively clean fuel involving little processing and being easily transportable via pipelines, natural gas requires compression or low temperatures if it is to be used for cars or other vehicles.

C Yet there is another problem with natural gas. It may produce less carbon dioxide than other fossil fuels, but the major stumbling block to its use is that the methane released lives for a long time in the atmosphere. In addition, as it is a non-renewable energy source like petroleum, in coming years natural gas will not be in use. But in the short term at least, the situation looks rosy.

D Ethanol, despite the drawback of a dearth of commercial outlets, heralds a new dawn for the energy market. But, before we consider ethanol in depth, let us look at hydrogen. It is perhaps the most attractive of all renewable fuels. Its greatest appeal is that it is readily available everywhere in the form of water (H^2O). Solar energy is used to split the water into hydrogen and oxygen and then recombine it, with water being the waste by-product. Perhaps its main drawback is making the hydrogen production units small enough to fit cars. But once this happens, the future of hydrogen is bright indeed.

2 Scan the passage for the words in exercise 1, or other words with similar meanings, and underline them.

3 Study the table about the reading passage in exercise 1 and decide what kind of words are needed for each blank space.

Type of fuel	Main advantage	Main disadvantage	Future
Petroleum	Very advanced infrastructure	**1** _____	Uncertain
Natural Gas	Relatively clean	Produces **2** _____	**3** _____
Ethanol		Lack of **4** _____	Signals a **5** _____
Hydrogen	**6** _____	Hydrogen production units for cars not small enough	**7** _____

4 Complete the table. Use no more than TWO words from the reading passage in exercise 1.

5 Look at the table below and insert four headings from the list in spaces 1–4.

> Method ■ Types of power ■ Types of organization ■ Types of environmental risks
> Location ■ Homes supplied ■ Environmental impact

1 _____	**2** _____	**3** _____	**4** _____
south coast	wave	high	sufficient for 26,000
mouth of river	tidal	low	sufficient for 15,000
at sea	wind	low	sufficient for 31,000

6 What other words do you know for the nouns *method*, *types*, and *impact*?

7 In your own words, briefly describe the information relating to the table in exercise 5 above.

Completing flow charts

1 Flow chart tasks normally relate to processes or sequences. Match each linking device below with a stage from the flow chart in exercise 2 opposite. Which can relate to any stage? Which cannot relate to any stage? The first one has been done for you.

firstly ____*stage one*____   finally _____

thirdly _____   at first _____

after that _____   in the next phase _____

subsequently _____   following that _____

simultaneously _____

2 The flow chart below is taken from a Flow chart completion task. Skim the chart, predict the type of word and where possible the words themselves to complete the chart.

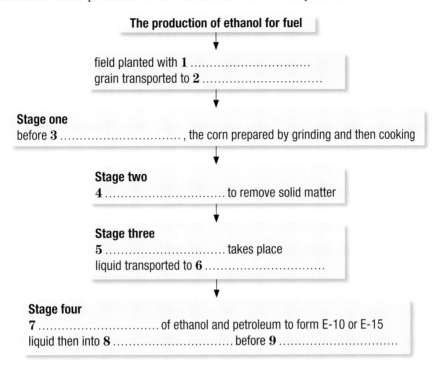

The production of ethanol for fuel

field planted with **1** ....
grain transported to **2** ....

Stage one
before **3** ...., the corn prepared by grinding and then cooking

Stage two
4 .... to remove solid matter

Stage three
5 .... takes place
liquid transported to **6** ....

Stage four
7 .... of ethanol and petroleum to form E-10 or E-15
liquid then into **8** .... before **9** ....

3 Now complete the chart using no more than TWO WORDS from the passage below.

The production of fuel-ethanol or 'grain spirit' from grain is relatively straightforward. It is made from harvested crops. As the demand for alternative 'clean' fuels increases, farmers are switching from planting crops for consumption to fuel crops like corn, barley, wheat or others that produce oil like palm and rape seed. The growing process is no different from that of any

5   crop. A farmer simply plants a field of corn, which is then harvested. Instead of being taken to a mill to produce flour, the corn is delivered by lorry to a distillery where it goes through four main stages before it can be used as fuel. First, during a preparation phase, the grain is ground and then cooked prior to the fermentation process commencing. Then, before the distillation of the liquid to produce the ethanol takes place, solid matter has to be removed by filtration. At a fuel-

10 ethanol plant, the blending of ethanol and petroleum is carried out to produce E-10, a mix of 10 per cent ethanol and 90 per cent petroleum, or E-15, which is 15 per cent ethanol and 85 per cent petroleum. The liquid is then put into storage and the distribution process is ready to begin.

4 Turn sentences a–e into notes as in the flow chart above.
  a Diamonds are formed deep below the surface of the Earth.
  b Filtration is followed by fermentation.
  c Heat is generated by the waste buried in the ground.
  d Electricity is generated by the rotating blades.
  e The recording is published, sold and played on the radio.

Technique
Notice the form of the words in flow charts. Stages in a flow chart are often expressed in note form. Example: Ethanol is produced once the filtering is completed. → *Ethanol produced once filtering completed.*

Improve your IELTS word skills

1 Complete the following descriptions by inserting the verbs in the correct tense. Choose from present active, present passive or infinitive with *to*.

store ▪ react ▪ filter ▪ distribute ▪ extract ▪ blend

Firstly, plant seeds are crushed **1** _____ the oil. Then this oil **2** _____ to take out the impurities. Next, hydrogen is added to it under high pressure. This hydrogen **3** _____ with the oil and makes it hard. Following this, the oil **4** _____ with other vegetable oils. Finally, the margarine **5** _____ in tubs until it **6** _____ to the shops.

fix ▪ carry ▪ grow ▪ fall ▪ spread

A seed **7** _____ from a tree to the forest floor or **8** _____ along by the wind, or by a bird or other animal. Lying dormant until the arrival of spring, the seed then sprouts roots **9** _____ it to the ground. The seed begins **10** _____ and in time develops into a fragile sapling. Eventually, the sapling grows into a tree, whose seeds in turn **11** _____ by the wind.

emerge (x2) ▪ live ▪ lay ▪ grow ▪ become

An adult mosquito **12** _____ its eggs in water. Larvae **13** _____ from the eggs after 48 hours. They **14** _____ and **15** _____ in the water. Eventually each larva **16** _____ a pupa. An adult mosquito **17** _____ from each pupa within about two days.

cool ▪ destroy ▪ heat ▪ gain

In the process known as pasteurization, milk **18** _____ to a temperature of about 72°C. Then it **19** _____ immediately. In this way, bacteria in the milk **20** _____ and the milk **21** _____ a longer shelf life.

2 Which texts describe a life cycle and which describe a production process? Create a suitable title for each text.

3 Change the verbs in the first two passages of exercise 1 into nouns. Be careful with the spelling.

Reading Passage 3

1 You should spend 20 minutes on questions 1–14 which are based on Reading Passage 3.

Coffee rust

Why do the British drink so much tea? The answer to this question can be traced back, unexpectedly, to a humble fungus, *hemileia vastatrix*, which attacks the leaves of coffee plants causing a disease

5 popularly known as coffee rust. The appearance of this disease was first reported in the British colony of Ceylon (now Sri Lanka) in 1867. Over the next twenty years, coffee production in Asia and Africa was virtually wiped out. Following a period of severe

10 economic and social upheaval, planters in British colonies shifted to planting tea, and the British were gradually transformed into a nation of tea drinkers.

Under British rule, the island of Ceylon was stripped of its forests to turn over every available acre to coffee production. By the 1870s, Ceylon was exporting nearly 100 million pounds of coffee a year,

15 much of it to England. This empire, however, was swiftly devastated by the arrival of the coffee rust fungus. The rust organism can be recognized by the presence of yellowish powdery lesions on the undersides of the leaves of the coffee plant. Occasionally, green shoots and even the green coffee berries can be infected. The infected leaves drop prematurely, leaving long expanses of bare twigs. This defoliation causes shoots and roots to starve and consequently to die back, reducing the

20 number of nodes on which coffee can be produced the following season.

The rust fungus is dispersed by both wind and rain. By observing the patterns of infection on individual leaves, it can be deduced that splashing rain is the most important means of local, or short-range dispersal. Dispersal over wider areas is primarily by wind, although insects such as flies and wasps may also play a small part. How the fungus first made its way from its native Ethiopia to Ceylon is unknown,

25 but human intervention seems to be the only plausible explanation. Insects as carriers can be ruled out, and it is doubtful whether the fungus could have been blown so far.

The coffee growers probably hoped at first that the disease would disappear as quickly and unaccountably as it had begun. By 1879, however, it was clear that it was not going away, and the Ceylon government made an appeal for someone to be sent to help. The British government responded by

30 sending Harry Marshall Ward, whose brief was to investigate the coffee rust phenomenon and hopefully come up with a cure.

Ward recommended that to effectively protect the plant from invasion, the leaves should be treated with a coating of fungicide (lime-sulfur). Unfortunately, in the case of the Ceylon plantations, the rust epidemic was too well established for this protective measure to save the coffee trees. He also pointed

35 out the risks of intensive monoculture. The continuous planting of coffee trees over the island, without

even the benefit of windbreaks, had created a perfect environment for a fungus epidemic to spread. Despite Ward's warning, when the coffee trees were replaced with tea bushes, they were planted at the same density. It was only by good fortune that no similar fungus arrived to invade the tea bushes and that improved fungicides were soon available to protect the crop.

40 With the destruction of the coffee plantations in Ceylon and subsequent arrival of coffee rust in Java and Sumatra, the world's coffee production shifted to the Americas. Plantations were swiftly established in the tropical highlands of Brazil, Colombia and Central America. Brazil soon became the world's major coffee supplier, closely followed by Colombia.

Coffee rust was successfully excluded from the Americas for over 100 years by careful quarantine
45 measures. However, in 1970, the fungus was discovered in Brazil, again probably brought in accidentally by humans. Once the barrier of the oceans had been breached, wind dispersal came into play. Infected trees were isolated by creating an 80 km coffeeless 'safety zone' around the infected area, but within eighteen months the rust had jumped the gap in the direction of the prevailing winds. Today, the fungus has spread throughout all the coffee-growing areas, including
50 Colombia and the countries of Central America.

Fungicide applications are now part of the routine production practices on coffee plantations, despite the expense for small growers. Good cultural management, taking into account the density of planting and the climate, is also paramount. Rust-resistant strains of coffee have also been developed but the crop is of poorer quality. Unless a truly rust-resistant variety with more desirable genetic traits can be produced, coffee rust will have to be managed as a continuous epidemic on a perennial crop.

Questions 1–7

Complete the diagram below.

*Choose **NO MORE THAN THREE WORDS** from Reading Passage 3 for each answer.*

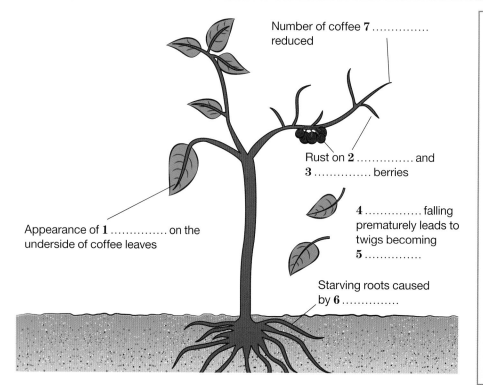

Number of coffee **7** .... reduced

Rust on **2** .... and **3** .... berries

4 .... falling prematurely leads to twigs becoming **5** ....

Appearance of **1** .... on the underside of coffee leaves

Starving roots caused by **6** ....

Technique

Labelling a diagram

1 Study the diagram and identify the type of word for each gap.

2 Underline scan words. Try to predict some of the answers.

3 Scan the reading passage to identify which section describes the information in the diagram. Is it likely to be at the beginning, in the middle or at the end of the reading passage?

4 Read the section carefully and complete the gaps, using the scan words to guide you to the answers.

5 Remember the sequence will probably follow the same order as the numbers on the diagram.

Questions 8 and 9

*Choose the correct letter, **A**, **B**, **C** or **D**.*

8 The most important means of long-range dispersal is

   A rain.

   B wind.

   C wasps.

   D flies.

9 Coffee rust spread easily in Ceylon

   A due to the density of the coffee trees.

   B due to the windbreaks.

   C because the fungicide didn't work.

   D because it was well established.

Questions 10–14

*Complete each sentence with the correct ending, **A–G**.*

10 The move of coffee production to the Americas was triggered by

11 Before 1970, American plantations were protected through

12 Attempts in the Americas to isolate the infected trees failed due to

13 The coffee trees now have to be protected continuously by

14 In the management of the coffee crops, it is also important to consider

   A the density of planting and the climate.

   B the application of fungicide.

   C the coffee rust devastation in Ceylon.

   D the increased demand for coffee in Europe.

   E careful quarantine measures.

   F the genetic traits of the coffee tree.

   G the prevailing winds.

Technique

Choose 5–7 words or phrases from the reading passage and the questions for future use in all skills. Record the words according to theme and/or function and with a context, e.g. Question 10 'was triggered by', which can be recorded under cause and effect.

2 Choose 5–7 words or phrases from the reading passage and the questions that you think will be useful to remember. Keep a record of them.

3 Make a list of the text features in this reading passage, e.g. description, historical information and problem. Then do the same with Reading passages 1 and 2.

UNIT AIMS

TOPIC	EXAM PRACTICE
Predicting	**Matching headings**
Answering Yes/No/Not Given statements (writer's claims)	**Answering Yes/No/Not Given statements (writer's claims)**
Matching headings (1)	**Completing multiple-choice questions**

Predicting

1 Look at the photos and answer questions a–d.

a How are the learning environments different in each picture? What other patterns of learning can you think of?

b Which of these ways of learning do you prefer? Why?

c Which pattern of learning has been most frequent in your education?

d Is the way people learn in the modern world changing? How?

e How do you think education will be different in the future? Give examples.

2 Read headings i–iv, taken from a Matching headings task, and answer questions a–d about the words in italic.

> **i** *Types* of jobs where literacy needed
>
> **ii** *Prediction* about developments
>
> **iii** The *reasons* behind illiteracy
>
> **iv** Illiteracy – a *problem* facing many advanced economies

a Which word relates to a general issue?

b Which word relates to causes?

c Which word relates to a future situation?

d Which words relate to categorizing information?

3 Read this explanation from a student predicting the order of the headings. Decide the correct sequence for i–iv in exercise 2.

> If you are writing about illiteracy in advanced economies, it is logical to state the general issue or problem first. Then, you say where it is found. After that, you can talk about the causes, and then what is going to happen next.

Technique

Learn to notice patterns in the reading passages in IELTS. Notice their features such as problem and solution, cause and effect, general and specific within passages. Also take note of the features and the organization of whole passages. This will help you to predict the order of headings, making it easier for you to navigate reading passages. You will be faster at answering the questions.

4 Read headings i–iv taken from a Matching headings task and answer questions a–d.

> i   A problem faced by education systems in advanced nations
> ii The importance of the state in providing education
> iii The influence of private enterprise
> iv The impact of recent change

a   Which heading relates to an effect or consequence?
b   Which headings relate to causes?
c   Which heading contains an indefinite article? Why?
d   What does the heading containing an indefinite article relate to?

5 Based on the headings in exercise 4, which of these descriptions best fits the likely pattern of the article?

a   The writer begins by stating the effects of a problem. Then the writer gives a description of the problem. Finally, the writer details its causes.
b   The writer begins by stating the problem. Then the writer gives details of the factors which contribute to this problem. Finally, the writer describes the consequences.

6 Find an example of a text which contains a problem and solution(s). Use the Internet or look in magazines or books.

7 Make a list of the benefits of prediction and add to the list as you prepare for the IELTS exam.

> **Technique**
> Keep a checklist of text features, especially those that fit together: problem and solution, cause and effect, classification, examples, explanation, description, process. Skim your checklist before you look at reading passages as you prepare for the exam.

Answering Yes/No/Not Given statements (writer's claims)

1 Statements 1–7 below are taken from a Yes/No/Not Given task. Read the statements, and then answer questions a–d.

> 1   Some journalists take the view that more British schoolchildren should study languages.
> 2   The number of English speakers worldwide makes it unnecessary for British tourists to learn languages.
> 3   Only British teenagers find languages boring.
> 4   British teenagers' reluctance to learn languages is linked to the availability of films and music in English.
> 5   In the past, studying French made it easier for British people to learn further languages.
> 6   The lack of linguistic skills within British companies has resulted in business being lost.
> 7   American businesspeople are less interested in learning languages than British businesspeople.

> **Technique**
> Yes/No/Not Given questions are similar to True/False/Not Given, but they are used in passages where the writer is presenting a claim or opinion. Collect a list of different examples of statements that relate to claims. This will help you to see the type of language that is used.

a   Which statements contain a comparison?
b   Which contain a cause and effect?
c   Which contain words with negative connotations? Underline them.
d   Using the title of the passage in exercise 2 on page 32 and the information from your answers to questions a–c above, can you predict which statements are True/False/Not Given? Make a note of your predictions.

2 For each of the statements 1–7 in exercise 1, decide if they agree with the writer's claims (Yes) or contradict (No) the writer's claims in the following reading passage. Write 'Not Given' if it is impossible to say what the writer thinks about this.

An answer to the belief that British people cannot learn languages

A Every so often, the educational supplements of our broadsheets devote an entire issue to the danger the British face of falling behind in Europe because so few of our schoolkids speak foreign languages. Most recently, the German ambassador lambasted us for only ever speaking English, a rebuke echoed by his French and Spanish counterparts.

B The truth is that foreign languages are phenomenally unpopular in secondary schools. Poor teaching and the late introduction of the subject are often cited as the main reasons youngsters are so loath to study them. Another factor for our notorious laziness vis-à-vis other tongues has to be that we are brought up to believe that the whole world speaks English, so why bother? Why indeed? Struggling to communicate in another language is, for all but the committed and enthusiastic linguist, a frustrating experience, which, if not necessary, is best avoided. And yes, when millions of Brits take their annual holidays abroad, local tourism, travel, catering and retail staff are all trained in at least rudimentary English. So, again, there is little motivation to learn more than a couple of words.

All this is true, and yet illuminates only part of the picture. British teenagers are generally bored by French or German verbs, but the underlying reasons are more complex than a vague assumption that they only need to speak English because everyone else does. Their leisure activities revolve around pop music, sport, computers, television and films. These things are already in English; translations and subtitles are the exception. Furthermore, the most powerful country in the world happens to speak our language, and we absorb its cultural exports easily and readily. So, for us, language is not a major issue.

C Of course, should the world situation change, and the United States become a Hispanic country, as some boffins have predicted, the British would see the benefit of learning Spanish and do so. Not so long ago, knowledge of French was more widespread here, and eagerly acquired, when that language was of paramount international importance.

D The belief that we will lag behind our European business partners also needs to be dissected. The canard here is that we lose out because our businessmen and women can't keep up with the local lingo. But surely, it is competitiveness and the attraction of lucrative offers that count. After all, American executives don't wring their hands at their lack of linguistic skills.

3 Check if any of your predictions in exercise 1d were correct.

Matching headings (1)

1 Decide which three nouns are the odd ones out in the list below and explain why.

> doctor ■ effect ■ impact ■ table ■ problem ■ consequence ■ benefit ■ solution ■ prediction
> skyscraper ■ example ■ description ■ factor ■ reason ■ argument

2 Match the general nouns 1–4 with sections A–D in the reading passage opposite.

1 The belief   **2** The consequence   **3** Reasons   **4** A criticism

3 Complete the headings in exercise 2 above by choosing an appropriate ending from a–f below.

a that business lost due to lack of linguistic ability disproved
b why young British people learn languages
c why young people don't learn languages
d of English not being a major language
e why foreign language learning disliked
f of British attitudes to learning languages

4 Sentences a–f give techniques for doing Matching headings tasks. These were listed by a student revising for the IELTS reading. Which do you think is the most important? Why?

a Skim the headings for a summary of the passage.
b Scan the text using the general nouns like *effects*, *problem*, etc and also synonyms of these nouns.
c Scan for words in the heading which help locate the information.
d Predict the likely position in the passage for some of the paragraph headings.
e Read and match each paragraph in turn, thinking of the writer's overall purpose.
f Check that the sequence of paragraphs makes sense.

5 A student skimmed three paragraphs 1–3, paying attention only to the words which give meaning. Quickly skim the words he looked at below, and decide which title, a or b, is better in each case.

1 Formal education – academic or vocational – obviously of value – however – education outside formal school – greater impact on individual – main criticism of schools/universities: don't prepare students for work – many people successful without formal education – informal education influences countless businessmen/women – Einstein, left school when sixteen – other self-taught people – formal education considered as stifling entrepreneurs – not providing skills in all fields – no problem going straight into work even after basic education – learn on the job.
  a The importance of academic education
  b The impact of education outside formal settings

2 Education – different forms – formal from primary to university – vocational – students learn work-related skills, e.g. construction/ engineering/catering or apprentices – trainees learn while working – e.g. with experienced plumbers, etc. – in UK/many other countries latter generally considered inferior – but now apprenticeships important – lack of skilled workers in construction driving up demand.
  a Different types of education
  b A skills-based approach to education

3 Education radically different in future: autonomy of the learner will be central – teachers disappear – replaced by robots/machines – transmit knowledge and skills directly to the brain – languages/musical instruments – data transmission via satellite to human brain.
  a Future developments in education
  b Learning languages in the future

Technique

Notice that by looking at a few words it is possible to select a heading for the paragraph. The skimmed words help to give the theme and gist of the paragraph. The other words you use for close, careful reading. Look again at page 14 in Unit 2.

Improve your IELTS word skills

1 Make the following adjectives negative by adding the prefixes *un-*, *in-*, *dis-*, *im-*, *il-*, *ir-*, *a-*.

> ambitious ■ conscious ■ accurate ■ literate ■ mortal ■ replaceable ■ relevant
> similar ■ satisfied ■ symmetrical ■ political

Technique

Academic texts may use a number of words that you have not seen before. If the word contains a prefix, you can often work out the meaning, for example: *an unimportant* (= not important) *pastime, the unborn* (= not yet born) *citizens.*

2 Complete the following sentences using the negative form of one of the above adjectives.

a Coral reefs are _____ . Once they are destroyed, they are gone forever.

b If the patient remains _____ , he should be put in the recovery position.

c Some students do not see the point of studying history as they find it _____ to the modern world.

d The two students' background was not _____ as they both came from working-class families.

e Unfortunately, the data was wrongly analysed and some of the figures were _____ .

f Although doctors and nurses generally prefer to be _____ , all of them are united against the government in this matter.

g No form of life on this planet can be _____ since our Sun's lifespan will end in a few billion years.

h Low status jobs tend to attract _____ workers, which makes it difficult to raise the skills level among the staff.

i The regularity of the layout of the 16th century garden was replaced by more _____ shapes.

3 Use your knowledge of prefixes to work out the meanings of the words in italics in sentences a–k.

a 'Awkward' is one of the most frequently *misspelt* words in English.

b The health service has been drastically *underfunded* for the last ten years.

c There are plans for the rail industry to be *denationalized*.

d Some environmentalists are concerned about the effect of *overfishing* on our oceans.

e Students who fail the exam will have a chance to *resit* the following year.

f The growth in obesity among young people means that a significant number of parents will *outlive* their children.

g By 1950, sales had reached almost three times the *pre-war* level.

h Pericles was perhaps the first Greek leader who was truly *pro-democracy*.

i The drug is believed to have a strong *anti-aggressive* effect.

j Investments reached a *post-crisis* peak last month.

k The machine was badly damaged in the storm and is now *unusable*.

Reading Passage 4

1 You should spend 20 minutes on questions 1–13 which are based on Reading Passage 4.

Questions 1–7

*The reading passage has nine paragraphs, **A–I**.*

*Choose the best headings for paragraphs **B–H** from the list of headings below.*

List of headings

i   The effect of emphasis on short-term educational goals

ii   The limited effects of music

iii   The future of music

iv   Benefits for health

v   The effects of early exposure to music

vi   The skills involved in musical activity

vii   A playwright's perception of music

viii   Early exposure to music in the USA

ix   Music without instruments

x   The 'Mozart effect'

xi   Order or chaos

xii   The creation of The Voices Foundation

xiii   A method for training singers

xiv   The use of music in Shakespeare's plays

Example Paragraph A xi

1   Paragraph B

2   Paragraph C

3   Paragraph D

4   Paragraph E

5   Paragraph F

6   Paragraph G

7   Paragraph H

Example Paragraph I iii

Technique

1 Skim the headings to form a general idea of the topic. Note repeated words.

2 Skim the reading passage and the other questions. Why is there no heading for the reading passage?

3 Identify and underline the general nouns in the headings. Look for connections and logical orderings between the nouns.

4 Read any examples given and make sure you do not cross them out. Make a note that they are already used.

4 Make predictions about which paragraph each heading relates to.

5 Skim the paragraphs to check your predictions and complete the matching exercise.

6 Check your answers by reading your headings in order.

Technique

Always read examples and skim the relevant paragraphs for the examples. They help you with the organization of the reading passage.

A Even the Greeks couldn't agree about it. Was music a source of order and proportion in society, regulating its innate chaos in ways similar to the disciplines of geometry and architecture? Or did its ability to express passionate emotions beyond the reach of words create the potential for disorder and anarchy? Compare the behaviour of an audience listening to classical string quartets with headbangers at a rave, and the age-old conflict between Apollo and Dionysus is made manifest all over again in our own time.

B Shakespeare, though, came clean. For him, 'the man who hath no music in himself, Nor is not mov'd with concord of sweet sounds, Is fit for treasons, stratagems and spoils; The motions of his spirit are dull as night …' Throughout his plays, Shakespeare perceives music as a healing force, an art whose practice makes man whole.

C Yet, despite the growth of the science of music therapy within the last two centuries, and despite the huge weight of books published on the miraculous 'Mozart effect', our schools and colleges have fallen strangely silent. The so-called 'Mozart effect' presents anecdotal and statistical evidence for advances in both social and academic skills in those children exposed in their formative years to the music of Mozart. But, in an age obsessed by pragmatism and by short-term vocational learning, music has been marginalized in both primary and secondary education. Compared with the holy trinity of reading, writing and arithmetic, music is regarded as an unimportant pastime. As a result, children are leaving school not only totally ignorant of their own musical heritage, but lacking in social, physical and mental skills which musical performance can uniquely promote.

D Playing an instrument requires a degree of concentration and coordination which brings into play a plethora of mental and physical skills which are being eroded in our push-button world. Socialization and teamwork are also involved. Schools with wind bands, string ensembles, jazz groups and orchestras are right up there at the top of the league tables. In excelling in musical activity, the students' performance in many other fields of learning is refocused and radically improved.

E There are medical aspects too. Long before British primary schools discovered the recorder – that most basic of all modern woodwind instruments – Australian Aborigines had developed the didgeridoo. Like the clarinet and the flute, this haunting and beautiful instrument helped to overcome both upper and lower respiratory tract problems and encouraged better sleep. In playing a wind instrument, abdominal muscles are used to support the breathing system. And these are the very muscles which come into play when an asthmatic is experiencing an attack.

F But what of those individuals and schools which simply cannot afford a musical instrument? What of those institutions where not a single member of staff can read music? This is where the human being's most primitive form of music-making comes into its own. Singing is free. Everyone possesses a voice. And, with it, the body expresses itself in the most fundamental and organic way.

G The Hungarian composer Zoltan Kodaly knew this, and developed his own system of training ear and voice within a simple yet comprehensive system of body language. Today, an organization called The Voices Foundation adapts and applies Kodaly's methods, aiming to give children back their singing voices, and to make our schools ring with music-making once again. Their advisors and teachers have already achieved extraordinary turn-around effects the length and breadth of Britain and in schools in the troubled areas of South Africa.

H Important work is currently being done in Finland, Israel and the United States on pre-school, even pre-birth, musical education. Music in the womb is very much part of the life of the unborn future citizens of Finland. And one has only to look at the educational standards, health records and professional musical activity in this small nation to see what dividends music in education pays from the earliest days of human life.

I Mozart has been celebrated in his anniversary years of 1991 and again in 2006. By the time of the next Mozart-Year, shall we have allowed music to conjure a better society for us all? Or, relegated to the ranks of mere entertainment, will music be eroded of its unique power to heal and to make whole?

Technique

Make notes about text features in the margins of reading passages as you prepare for the IELTS. For example, aim to identify three to five text features such as examples, effects, results, methods, future developments, etc. In time, you will notice these automatically. In the exam itself, you may not have time to do this.

Questions 8–10

Do the following statements agree with the claims of the writer in the reading passage?

Write

YES	*if the statement agrees with the writer's claims*
NO	*if the statement contradicts the writer's claims*
NOT GIVEN	*if it is impossible to say what the writer thinks about this*

8   In Shakespeare's dramas, music is seen in a positive light.

9   Schools lack the funds to buy luxury items like musical instruments.

10   Musical activity can only lead to a slight improvement in children's social, physical and mental skills.

> **Technique**
>
> Think about the words that help you to focus on the meaning of the claims, not just words that help you scan: 8 *positive* 9 *lack* 10 *only/slight*. Each of these words qualifies the statement in some way. To see how important these words are, turn the statements into questions. These words carry the main stress.

Questions 11–13

*Choose the correct letter, **A**, **B**, **C** or **D**.*

11   According to the writer, studying music

   A   may not help all students to improve in other areas of their studies.

   B   means that students spend less time on reading, writing and arithmetic.

   C   helps students to improve enormously in other areas of their studies.

   D   means that students will excel as professional musicians.

12   The didgeridoo is an instrument that

   A   has a negative effect on those suffering with breathing problems.

   B   benefits those suffering with breathing problems.

   C   tends to send those who listen to it to sleep.

   D   sounds sad to most people.

13   Which of the following is the most suitable heading for Reading Passage 4?

   A   The growth of music in the school curriculum

   B   Music throughout the ages

   C   Music for everyone

   D   The beneficial effects of a musical education

2   Answer these questions.

   a   Which type of music do you prefer? Do you play an instrument? Which/Why?

   b   Do you like classical music? Why/Why not?

   c   Is it important to listen to different types of music?

   d   Do you think young people listen to music rather than play an instrument nowadays? Why/Why not?

UNIT AIMS

READING SKILLS
Completing summaries with wordlists
Selecting statements from a list
Answering global multiple-choice questions

EXAM PRACTICE
Completing summaries with wordlists
Completing multiple-choice questions

Completing summaries with wordlists

1 Look at the photo and answer questions a–d.

  a What aspect of modern life does the photo suggest?

  b To what extent is the gap between the capabilities of older and younger people real?

  c Do young people take on responsibilities at an earlier age than they did in the past? If so, is this a good development?

  d Which age group – young adult, middle aged, elderly – would you associate the adjectives below with? Explain why.

> creative analytical responsible curious
> flexible spontaneous sensible

2 Skim the title of the reading passage on page 39. What can you predict about the topic of the reading passage from the title?

3 Read the summary, which is taken from a Summary task with a wordlist. Then answer questions a and b below.

  a Which words in the summary will help you scan for the beginning and the end of the relevant section of the text?

  b Skim the reading passage and decide where the summary begins and ends.

> **Technique**
>
> Learn to work out whether the summary relates to part of a reading passage or a whole reading passage. For example, a summary with a heading is likely to relate to part of a passage. The rubric may also tell you which paragraphs the questions relate to, so always check the rubric.

According to a recent report, young people aged 8–18 are wasting
1 .... of time by multi-tasking. In fact, they are spending as much
as 50 per cent longer than if they did the same tasks **2** .... Some
young people are juggling a larger and larger array of **3** .... as
they study, while surfing the net, sending **4** .... , answering the
phone and listening to music simultaneously. Other studies have shown
that this **5** .... is affecting the way families operate, with young
people too self-absorbed to talk to other family members or to eat at the
family table. The electronic **6** .... is also apparently having a
7 .... on young people's studies and work.

Excessive demands on young people

Being able to multi-task is hailed by most people as a welcome skill, but not according to a recent study which claims that young people between the ages of eight and eighteen of the so-called 'Generation M' are spending a considerable amount of their time on fruitless efforts as they multi-task. It argues that, in fact, these young people are
5   frittering away as much as half of their time again as they would if they performed the very same tasks one after the other.

Some young people are juggling an ever larger number of electronic devices as they study. At the same time as they are working, young adults are also surfing the Internet, or sending out emails to their friends, and/or answering the telephone and listening to
10 music on their iPods or on another computer. As some new device comes along, it too is added to the list rather than replacing one of the existing devices.

Other research has indicated that this multi-tasking is even affecting the way families themselves function as young people are too wrapped up in their own isolated worlds to interact with the other people around them. They can no longer greet family
15 members when they enter the house, nor can they eat at the family table.

All this electronic wizardry is supposedly also seriously affecting young people's performance at university and in the workplace. When asked about their perception of the impact of modern gadgets on their performance of tasks, the overwhelming majority of young people gave a favourable response.

20 The response from the academic and business worlds was not quite as positive. The former feel that multi-tasking with electronic gadgets by children affects later development of study skills, resulting in a decline in the quality of writing, for example, because of the lack of concentration on task completion. They feel that many undergraduates now urgently need remedial help with study skills. Similarly, employers
25 feel that young people entering the workforce need to be taught all over again, as they have become deskilled.

While all this may be true, it must be borne in mind that more and more is expected of young people nowadays; in fact, too much. Praise rather than criticism is due in respect of the way today's youth are able to cope, despite what the older generation
30 throw at them.

4   Complete the summary in exercise 3 as far as you can without looking at the passage again. To what extent is it possible to predict the meaning of the missing words in the summary without reading the passage? Give reasons for your answer.

5 Complete the summary in exercise 3 using items A–M from the wordlist below.

Wordlist

A in sequence	**B** revolution	**C** beneficial effect
D much	**E** messages	**F** letters
G electronics	**H** negative impact	**I** electronic gizmos
J behaviour	**K** development	**L** significant amounts
M all together		

6 Using the following notes to help you, check the items you have selected from the wordlist for questions 1–7.

1 something to do with quantity
2 something to do with order
3 something to do with electronic things
4 something to do with things you send electronically
5 something to do with the way of doing things
6 something which has happened to do with electronics
7 something to do with the effect of 5 and 6

7 Underline the words in the reading passage which are paraphrases of the answers 1–7 above.

8 Make a checklist of techniques to help you complete summaries. Revise the checklist as you continue to prepare for the exam.

Selecting statements from a list

1 In the IELTS exam, you may be asked to select True statements from a list about a passage. Skim the statements about the reading passage on page 39 and answer questions a–c.

  a Which part of the passage do you think the answers are likely to be in?

  b Which statements can you predict to be true?

  c Which words can you use to scan? Can you use *electronic gadgets*? Why/Why not?

The list below gives some opinions about electronic gadgetry.

Which **THREE** opinions are mentioned by the writer of the text?

A According to students, electronic gadgets are now an inevitable part of the university landscape.

B Academics feel multi-tasking with electronic gadgets affects children's subsequent acquisition of study skills.

C Academics feel students are offered help with their writing and study skills.

D Most young people see no problems related to using electronic gadgets.

E Computer use at school fails to prepare students for academic life at university, according to academics.

F Employers feel that the use of electronic gadgets among children affects capacity to perform in the work environment.

G Employers think that overuse of computers and other gadgets definitely affects job prospects later in life.

> **Technique**
> Skim all of the statements when you have to select statements from a list. Try to predict possible answers after skimming the reading passage. Work out which part of the passage the statements relate to – the whole passage or just part of it. Use nouns/noun phrases to help you with the organization and functions of the reading passage.

2 Choose three opinions A–G mentioned by the writer in exercise 1. Use your predictions to help you.

Answering global multiple-choice questions

1 The question below is a Global multiple-choice question. Read the question and then answer questions a–c.

> *Choose the correct letter A, B, C or D.*
>
> The writer concludes that
>
> **A** the use of electronic gadgets at school is affecting academic study.
>
> **B** more is required of young people today and they cope well in the circumstances.
>
> **C** the use of electronic gadgets at school needs to be controlled.
>
> **D** electronic gadgets should be totally banned as they harm young people's job prospects.

a Look at the stem of the multiple-choice question. What does it tell you about the location of the answer?

b What does the title of the passage tell you about the writer's opinion?

c Which alternatives can you eliminate?

2 Using your answers to question 1, complete the Global multiple-choice question.

> **Technique**
> 1 Global multiple-choice questions can ask: about the purpose of the text, its source, about the writer's overall opinion, to choose the best title or to select the writer's conclusion.
>
> 2 Read the stem and the alternatives, remembering that the question refers to the whole text and not just a part of it, unless it is a conclusion.
>
> 3 Do not start re-reading a specific part of the text, as this may confuse you, again unless it is the conclusion. If you are really stuck, for all types of global questions, look at the conclusion.
>
> 4 Do not do this type of question before you have answered all the others.

Unit 5

Improve your IELTS word skills

1 Which of the following suffixes are used to form nouns and which are used to form adjectives?

-al ▪ -ic ▪ -ion ▪ -ment ▪ -ing

2 Find words in the reading passage on pages 43 and 44 that end with the suffixes listed in exercise 1.

3 Add the suffixes in exercise 1 to the following words to form nouns. You may need to make some small spelling changes.

act ▪ detect ▪ fulfil ▪ train ▪ compete ▪ produce ▪ settle

4 Add the suffixes in exercise 1 to the following words to form adjectives. You may need to make some small spelling changes.

strategy ▪ energy ▪ democracy ▪ habit ▪ benefit ▪ influence

5 Add the correct suffix to the words below. Decide if the words become nouns or adjectives.
-ful -less -al -ous

courage ▪ deny ▪ price ▪ use ▪ survive ▪ wonder ▪ worth

6 Complete the text by adding suffixes to the words in brackets.

A workforce made up entirely of young people is not necessarily the key to success and there is a growing **1** _____ (aware) among employers of the special **2** _____ (contribute) that older people can make. Yet while attitudes in the workplace may have changed, it seems that the **3** _____ (advertise) industry continues to look the other way. TV advertisements still often show older people in a negative or **4** _____ (stereotype) way and tend to feature younger users.

This, however, makes no sense. Older people usually have a higher income than the young and it is fairly easy to adjust the image of a product to make it more **5** _____ (attract) to them.

For example, mobile phones can be presented as a way to maintain **6** _____ (friend) across distances, a welcome **7** _____ (propose) to older people who often fear **8** _____ (lonely) in their later years. Showing more older people using a product not only makes good **9** _____ (finance) sense but it can also play a wider role in society in general by challenging age **10** _____ (discriminate).

Reading passage 5

You should spend 20 minutes on questions 1–13, which are based on Reading Passage 5.

Youth: The Future of Travel

Young people are invariably at the leading edge of change and innovation –
and the travel industry is no exception. Young people think outside the box,
push boundaries and experiment with the new. In an era of unprecedented
challenge for the travel industry, youth travel represents not just an important
5   market segment, but also a vital resource for innovation and change.

The travel industry is itself undergoing rapid change. Traditional vertical
distribution chains are giving way to a more complex value network
involving a wide range of different suppliers from within and beyond the
travel sector. Travel is no longer solely dependent on the infrastructure of
10   the old economy – airline seats, hotel beds and travel agents' shelves. We
are entering a new, flexible, networked economy in which information and
communications technology (ICT), local culture and society, education,
work and play have become part of the tourism value chain. In fact, the
inter-relationships between travel, other economic sectors and society as a whole have become
15   so integrated that we might conceive of a 'value web' rather than the old value chain.

New value web
In the new tourism value web, value is created by linking actors inside and outside the tourism sector in
different combinations to create and exploit new opportunities. Young people are often at the forefront
of such innovation, because they are willing to cross boundaries and make new links. As early-adopting,
20   heavy users of new technology, young people are pioneering the use of social networking sites and mobile
media in searching for travel information and purchasing products.

Young people are the future of travel
Youth travel has grown rapidly in recent decades as living standards have risen and the populations
of developing countries are starting to travel for the first time. Indeed, these first-time travellers are
25   often characterized by being young and comparatively affluent. The global youth travel industry is now
estimated to represent almost 190 million international trips a year, and the youth travel industry has
grown faster than global travel overall. By 2020 there will be almost 300 million international youth trips
per year, according to UNWTO forecasts.

The youth market therefore represents a major opportunity for future growth in the travel industry. With
30   effective development and marketing, the potential of the youth market can be increased still further.

Why youth travel is important
Youth travel is important because it is a market for the future – not just for the future development of the
young people themselves, but also the places they visit. WYSE Travel Confederation research shows that
young travellers often spend more than other tourists and they are likely to return and give more value
35   to the destination over their lifetime. Moreover, young travellers are a growth market globally, while the
spending power of older generations in Western economies may decline in the long term. Another reason
why young people are important is that they are less likely to be discouraged from travelling by factors
such as disease or natural disasters. They are also the pioneers who discover new destinations and are at
the cutting edge of using new technology. Last but not least, young travellers gain cultural benefits from
40   their travel, and contribute to the places they visit.

UNWTO and WYSE Travel Confederation are convinced that youth travel has moved far beyond its original status as a specialized travel niche to become an important element of the travel mix in any tourism destination. One of the reasons for this is that travel underpins many different aspects of youth lifestyles. For young people:

45   · Travel is a form of learning
· Travel is a way of meeting other people
· Travel is a way of getting in touch with other cultures
· Travel is a source of career development
· Travel is a means of self-development
50   · Travel is part of their identity – you are where you've been.

Young people see travel as an essential part of their everyday lives, rather than just a brief escape from reality. This has far-reaching consequences for the places they visit. Because of the way they travel, the social and cultural consequences of hosting young people are becoming even more important than the economic effects. So the added value to be extracted from youth travel lies in innovation, positioning,
55   cultural links, international trade and exchange, social support, education, learning support for local communities, and so on.

Questions 1–7

Complete the summary below using the list of words, (A–O) from the box below.

Youth travel: a force for change

In all fields, including the travel industry, young people are usually at the forefront of any new **1** .... They set trends and so are a **2** .... for innovation and change. This is important as the travel industry is also experiencing its own **3** .... The modern travel industry is not about airline seats and hotel beds any more, but a new more open economy where factors such as local culture and society have a **4** .... in tourism. Indeed, the **5** .... of travel and other parts of the economy and society means that traditional vertical distribution chains have been replaced by a **6** ...., or value web. Due to increased numbers of fairly rich young travellers from developing countries, **7** .... now accounts for nearly 190 million trips annually.

A transformation	**B** impact	**C** developments
D transforming	**E** crucial force	**F** conflict
G interest	**H** block	**I** role
J network	**K** link	**L** older travellers
M integration	**N** circumstances	**O** youth travel

Technique

Summary with wordlist

1 Scan the reading passage for the section which relates to the summary.

2 Skim the summary and try to complete the spaces with your own words.

3 Look for words/ideas from the list that collocate with words in the text.

4 Find words/phrases in the list which are opposites. Find words that you can eliminate from the list.

5 Read the relevant section of the text and complete the answers.

6 Look at the end of the summary for clues about where the summary might end in the reading passage.

7 Note that some of the words in the summary answers may be the same as in the passage.

Questions 8–10

*Choose three letters, **A**–**G**.*

Which **THREE** of the following reasons for the importance of youth travel are given by the writer of the text?

A   They make use of the latest technology that is available.

B   They spend a large proportion of their money on travelling worldwide.

C   They avoid conflicts with local people more than older people.

D   They will probably return to the places they have visited later in their lives.

E   They are more likely to learn the local language than older people are.

F   They are experiencing a rapid increase in their disposable income.

G   They give something back to the destinations they have been to.

Questions 11–13

*Choose the correct letter, **A**, **B**, **C** or **D**.*

11 Travel is central to young people's lifestyle, partly because

    A   it helps them to relax.

    B   it is an educational experience.

    C   it improves their confidence.

    D   it makes them more mature.

12 According to the writer, the economic impact of hosting young people is

    A   of no consequence compared to the social and cultural effects.

    B   of greater consequence than the social and cultural effects.

    C   of lesser consequence than the social and cultural effects.

    D   just as valuable as the social and cultural effects.

13 The writer concludes that

    A   youth travel is not an important area for the travel industry.

    B   the main contribution of young people to the travel industry is in innovation.

    C   young people value the cultural links gained from travelling more than anything else.

    D   there is a wide range of additional benefits to be derived from youth travel.

2 What is your reaction to the contents of the reading passage? Do you agree with the reasons given for why travel is important for young people? Why/Why not?

6 Culture

UNIT AIMS

READING SKILLS
Using general nouns
Matching headings (2)
Matching information to paragraphs (1)
Matching information to names

EXAM PRACTICE
Matching headings
Matching information to names
Completing multiple-choice questions
Completing global multiple-choice questions

Using general nouns

1 Look at the photos and answer questions a–c.

a   What aspects of culture do the pictures reflect?
b   Do you associate the word 'culture' with the activities shown? Why/Why not?
c   Which factors in the box are important in making your culture different from other people's? Give examples for each item you choose.

> food ■ sport ■ music ■ family ■ art ■ work

Technique

Learn to notice and collect general nouns as IELTS reading questions often contain such words. These nouns belong to a limited set. By identifying these, it is easier to find the answer.

2 Divide the following general nouns into pairs with similar meanings.

> advantage ■ aim ■ benefit ■ consequence ■ difference
> difficulty ■ discrepancy ■ factor ■ hazard ■ influence
> outcome ■ problem ■ purpose ■ risk

3 General nouns are common in matching tasks. Complete each of the paragraph headings below with a suitable word from the box.

> action ■ reservations ■ role ■ strategies ■ outline ■ problem

a   The _____ played by the individual in maintaining traditions
b   The _____ of protecting culture from outside influences
c   Different _____ to combat vandalism of historical sites
d   _____ about the benefits of globalization
e   _____ taken to improve historical sites of international importance
f   An _____ of various strategies to promote the speaking of Chinese

4 Describe in your own words the possible paragraph contents of three headings in exercise 3.

Matching headings (2)

1 Read the paragraph headings i-vi and answer questions a–d below.

> **i** Various interpretations of culture based on meaning
>
> **ii** The problem of explaining what culture means
>
> **iii** A definition of culture based on shared behaviour
>
> **iv** Defining a culture is not only a matter of observation
>
> **v** The main reason for difficulty in investigating culture
>
> **vi** The discrepancy between personal explanations and the real reasons for cultural behaviour

a What do you think the topic of the text is?
b Which general nouns are used in the headings? Underline them.
c Based on your answers to a and b, which is the most likely heading for paragraph A on page 48?
d What does the plural in the word *interpretations* indicate?

2 Skim the passage on page 48 and match each paragraph A–D with a heading from i–vi above. Decide why the remaining two headings are not suitable.

3 The diagram shows the plan of a paragraph. Decide which paragraph from the passage it relates to. Underline the three examples mentioned.

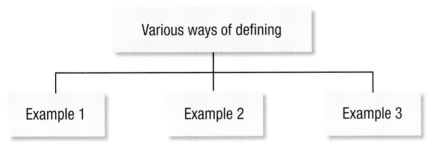

Various ways of defining

Example 1   Example 2   Example 3

Matching information to paragraphs (1)

1 Underline the general nouns in each phrase 1–4 below. Then decide which phrase is most likely to relate to a whole paragraph and explain why.

> **1** the idea that researching a culture is not just about observation
>
> **2** the fact that countries close to each other can be dissimilar
>
> **3** the fact that theories about culture can take a long time to develop
>
> **4** various anthropologists' ways of looking at the concept of culture

Technique

Notice and collect general nouns in Matching information to paragraph tasks. Compare these nouns to those used in Matching headings to paragraphs and sections in a reading passage. They are very similar.

2 Which paragraph (A–D) in the reading passage contains the information in 1–4?

The meaning of culture

A Culture is a term for which it is very difficult to give a precise meaning. The word means so many different things to different people, so devising a single acceptable definition is more problematic than may be first thought. The idea of culture as something shared is inherently complex. Even people neighbouring each other, or sharing a common language, or possessing certain common core values may actually have as many differences as similarities.

B Anthropologists have proposed over one hundred different definitions. A number of these are variations on the idea that culture consists of 'shared patterns of behaviour' as may be observed by the researcher. This is the definition put forward by Margaret Mead, for example, in her study of indigenous ritual in Samoa. This kind of definition, however, does not take account of the fact that studying culture is not just a question of observation. It also involves studying the meaning of this observed behaviour.

C Accordingly, other anthropologists, such as Max Weber, speak of culture as consisting of systems of shared meaning; as he puts it, 'man is an animal suspended in webs of significance he himself has spun.' Similarly, Claude Levi-Strauss also speaks of culture as a product of the implicit beliefs which underlie it. The problem with this approach is that the meaning of cultural behaviour is not always easy to establish. Explanations may be offered up to a point, but the underlying assumptions often remain obscure. Indeed, they are often not understood by insiders. As Chris Argyris and Donald Schon point out, what people say to explain their cultural behaviour and what really drives this behaviour are often

widely different. The search for meaning can therefore be a long and painstaking process, involving long periods of observation and interviews in order to build possible theories.

D While there are some cultures which have remained isolated for long periods of time, many others have built up commercial links with other groups. Eventually, this may lead to adopting elements of the other group's rituals and behaviour which then become integrated into those of the original group. Some cultures have clashed with less powerful neighbours only to find that over time their culture became heavily influenced by these subordinates, like the Romans by the Greeks. In this way, the original meaning of an aspect of cultural behaviour may be lost in history and may originally have been part of a belief system very different from that which prevails in the culture today. This dynamism is, perhaps, the major reason why researching the meaning behind cultural behaviour is far from easy.

3 Read this additional extract from the reading passage and answer the questions.

The study of a different culture can be carried out in different ways. It can be compared to the study of a new planet or terrain. We can study what is immediately observable: the valleys, mountains and different geographical features, or, in the case of a culture, the various rituals and patterns of behaviour. Alternatively, we can ask what values and beliefs underlie these behaviours or what past events have shaped them, just as we may ask what geological events have shaped the landscape. This deeper level of enquiry may often lead on to a third stage in which we not only assess the new culture, but we also become increasingly aware of the different factors which have created our own culture as well.

a What general noun in the first sentence means 'method'?
b What three methods are mentioned in the text?

4 Which of the phrases below relates to a part of the paragraph and which to the whole? Use the general nouns to help you decide.

i various strategies for studying another culture

ii a comparison between the study of a planet and a new culture

iii a cause of geographical features

Matching information to names

1 The lists below are taken from a task where you have to match information to names. Scan the previous reading passage on page 48 for the names and draw a box around each one.

1 Culture is something which is embodied in the way groups behave.

2 The reasons people give for their behaviour are often different from why it originally developed.

3 Societies create networks of meaning within which their members live.

4 Culture is something which arises from a group's beliefs.

List of people

A Margaret Mead

B Max Weber

C Claude Levi-Strauss

D Chris Argyris and Donald Schon

2 Match each statement 1–4 with the correct person A–D.

Improve your IELTS word skills

1 Decide which general nouns in the box below could replace the word in italics in this paragraph heading.

The *connection* between body language and environment.

link ■ bond ■ relationship ■ correlation ■ relation ■ strategy ■ association

2 The heading can also be rewritten in the form below. Which other verbs could be used? Use the list of nouns above to help you.

Example
How body language and environment are *connected*.

3 Divide the general nouns below into five groups with similar meanings.

aim ■ analysis ■ characteristic ■ consequence ■ difficulty ■ effect ■ explanation
feature ■ goal ■ interpretation ■ objective ■ obstacle ■ outcome ■ problem

4 Change the following sentences into paragraph headings using an appropriate general noun. Make the headings as short as you can.

Example
The paragraph exemplifies various subcultures in Brazilian society.
Various *examples* of Brazilian subcultures.

   a The paragraph describes the outcome of the research on stem cells.

   b The paragraph details how hydrogen is produced from water for energy.

   c The section explains how culture and wealth are linked.

   d The paragraph provides a list of the different factors involved in the production of a film.

   e The paragraph sets out the part played by the United Nations in protecting cultures under threat.

5 What synonyms can you find for the general nouns you used in a–e in exercise 4?

6 Using the nouns below, make headings that reflect aspects of a university student's life.

Example
Connection: The *connection* between studying and achievement

   1 Benefit: _____

   2 Aim: _____

   3 Problems: _____

   4 Ways: _____

   5 Examples: _____

   6 Factors: _____

   7 Effect: _____

Reading Passage 6

1 You should spend 20 minutes on questions 1–13, which are based on Reading
Passage 6.

Questions 1–4

*Reading Passage 6 has five sections, **A–E**.*

*Choose the correct heading for sections **B–E** from the list of
headings below.*

List of Headings

i   Research into African community life

ii   Views about intelligence in African societies

iii   The limitations of Western intelligence tests

iv   The Chinese concept of intelligence

v   The importance of cultural context in test design

vi   The disadvantages of non-verbal intelligence tests

vii   A comparison between Eastern and Western understanding
of intelligence

viii Words for 'intelligence' in African languages

ix   The impossibility of a universal intelligence test

Example Section **A iii**

1   Section B
2   Section C
3   Section D
4   Section E

Technique

1 Survey the whole
reading passage and
the questions.
2 Skim the title and
predict the contents
of the passage.
3 Skim the reading
passage in no more
than two minutes.
4 Skim the questions.
Use the questions to
help you improve your
understanding of the
general content of the
reading passage.

Technique

1 Do not just cross out
the example heading.
2 Skim the relevant
paragraphs for the
example(s), as this can
help you find the other
headings.
3 Skim the headings,
noticing the general
nouns such as views,
comparison, etc and
the words which help
you scan the text. Also
think of synonyms.
4 When you have
finished, check the
order of the headings
you have chosen and
see if they are logical.

Views of intelligence across cultures

A In recent years, researchers have found that
people in non-Western cultures often have
ideas about intelligence that are considerably
different from those that have shaped Western
5   intelligence tests. This cultural bias may
therefore work against certain groups of
people. Researchers in cultural differences in
intelligence, however, face a major dilemma,
namely: how can the need to compare people
10   according to a standard measure be balanced
with the need to assess them in the light of their
own values and concepts?

B For example, Richard Nesbitt of the University
of Michigan concludes that East Asian and
Western cultures have developed cognitive   15
styles that differ in fundamental ways, including
how intelligence is understood. People in
Western cultures tend to view intelligence as
a means for individuals to devise categories
and engage in rational debate, whereas   20
Eastern cultures see it as a way for members
of a community to recognize contradiction
and complexity and to play their social roles
successfully. This view is backed up by

Sternberg and Shih-Ying, from the University of Taiwan, whose research shows that Chinese conceptions of intelligence emphasize understanding and relating to others, and knowing when to show or not show one's intelligence.

C The distinction between East Asia and the West is just one of many distinctions that separate different ways of thinking about intelligence. Robert Serpell spent a number of years studying concepts of intelligence in rural African communities. He found that people in many African communities, especially in those where Western-style schooling is still uncommon, tend to blur the distinction between intelligence and social competence. In rural Zambia, for instance, the concept of *nzelu* includes both cleverness and responsibility. Likewise, among the Luo people in rural Kenya, it has been found that ideas about intelligence consist of four broad concepts. These are named *paro* or practical thinking, *luoro*, which includes social qualities like respect and responsibility, *winjo* or comprehension and *rieko*. Only the fourth corresponds more or less to the Western idea of intelligence.

D In another study in the same community, Sternberg and Grogorenko have found that children who score highly on a test of knowledge about medicinal herbs, a test of practical intelligence, often score poorly on tests of academic intelligence. This suggests that practical and academic intelligence can develop independently of each other, and the values of a culture may shape the direction in which a child's intelligence develops.

It also tends to support a number of other studies which suggest that people who are unable to solve complex problems in the abstract can often solve them when they are presented in a familiar context. Ashley Maynard, for instance, now professor of psychology at the University of Hawaii, conducted studies of cognitive development among children in a Mayan village in Mexico using toy looms, spools of thread and other materials drawn from the local environment. The research suggested that the children's development could be validly compared to the progression described by Western theories of development, but only by using materials and experimental designs based on their own culture.

E The original hope of many cognitive psychologists was that a test could be developed that was absent of cultural bias. However, there seems to be an increasing weight of evidence to suggest that this is unlikely. Raven's Progressive Matrices, for example, were originally advertised as 'culture free' but are now recognized as culturally loaded. Such non-verbal intelligence tests are based on cultural constructs which may not appear in a particular culture. It is doubtful whether cultural comparisons of concepts of intelligence will ever enable us to move towards creating a test which encompasses all aspects of intelligence as understood by all cultures. It seems even less likely that such a test could be totally free of cultural imbalance somewhere.

The solution to the dilemma seems to lie more in accepting that cultural neutrality is unattainable and that administering any valid intelligence test requires a deep familiarity with the relevant culture's values and practices.

Questions 5–9

Look at the following findings (Questions 5–9) and the list of reserarchers below.

*Match each finding with the correct researcher, **A–E**.*

List of findings

5   There is a clear relationship between intelligence and relationships with others in Chinese culture.

6   The difference between intelligence and social competence is not distinct in many African communities.

7   Children frequently scoring well in practical tests score less well in academic tests.

8   In experiments to measure cognitive development, there is a link between the materials used and the test results.

9   The way cognition is viewed in East Asian cultures differs fundamentally from those in Western cultures.

> **List of researchers**
> **A**   Richard Nesbitt   **B** Robert Serpell   **C** Ashley Maynard
> **D**   Sternberg and Shih-Ying   **E** Sternberg and Grogorenko

Technique

Matching names

1 Scan the passage for each name in the list.

2 Draw a box around each name. This limits where you need to look for their findings (opinions, claims, etc).

3 Skim to see whether the person's findings occur before or after their name. Then read the findings.

4 Read through the list of statements to find the correct match.

Question 10–12

The list below gives statements about non-verbal intelligence tests.

Which **THREE** statements are mentioned by the writer of the passage?

A   Raven's Progressive Matrices are widely considered to be culturally free.

B   Cultural comparisons will allow the development of culturally neutral tests.

C   The development of culturally neutral tests is unlikely.

D   Raven's Progressive Matrices are culturally specific.

E   The creation of culturally-free tests is sometimes possible.

F   Many cognitive psychologists originally hoped tests could be developed free of cultural bias.

Question 13

*Choose the correct letter, **A**, **B**, **C** or **D**.*

Which of the following is the main argument of the article?

A   Intelligence tests should include tests of social skills and responsibility.

B   Test takers from any culture can learn the cognitive style required by Western intelligence tests.

C   Intelligence tests cannot be free of cultural bias.

D   More research is needed to develop an intelligence test which is valid for all cultures.

2   Write down ways that (a) you (b) your friends (c) your family (d) people in your home country or a country you are familiar with use to measure intelligence in other people.

UNIT AIMS

READING SKILLS
Completing summaries without wordlists
Completing multiple-choice questions
Analysing questions

EXAM PRACTICE
Completing summaries without wordlists
Classifying information
Completing multiple-choice questions

Completing summaries without wordlists

1 Describe the photos and say which reflects your reading habits.

2 Answer the following questions about reading.

a How often do you read?
b What have you read today so far?
c Which types of books below do you like most? Give reasons.

> Romance ▪ Crime ▪ War ▪ Historical ▪ Biography ▪ Travel books
> Sci-fi ▪ Art books ▪ Science

d Some people think reading books will soon be a thing of the past. Do you agree?

3 Decide which are the best techniques from a–g to complete a Summary task without a wordlist.

a Skim and decide whether the missing words are adverbs, adjectives, nouns/noun phrases or verbs.
b Avoid thinking of your own words.
c Predict the meaning of the word in the blank space.
d Skim and ignore the blank space.
e Skim and say the word 'blank' for each missing word.
f Don't check your answers in the passage.
g Skim the summary first before you look at the passage.

4 Read the summary which relates to the reading passage on page 55. Using ONE word only from the passage, complete each space in the summary.

Most people join book clubs for **1** _____ reasons. The official reason is to discuss books, but members principally enjoy interacting with others in a **2** _____ atmosphere. Another reason for the popularity of book clubs is that reading is a **3** _____ pastime compared with cinema or theatre going. Some book clubs may **4** _____ on a particular genre, or they may decide to be **5** _____ in their choice of reading material. It all depends on the interest of the participants. Research suggests that the popularity of reading has remained **6** _____ since 1996, and it seems likely that the number of clubs will **7** _____ in the future.

Book clubs – from strength to strength

A The proliferation of book clubs, some 50,000 in the UK alone and who knows how many more worldwide, is quite a remarkable literary phenomenon. Participants of different ages and backgrounds gather on a weekly or monthly basis ostensibly to discuss books chosen by the
5 members, but the primary attraction for most people, and the factor behind the explosion in the number of groups, is not literary, but social. Human interaction with some added mental stimulation in a relaxed environment is integral to their success.

B The social aspect apart, the spread of book clubs can also be attributed to the low cost and the availability
10 of books, and the fact that compared to, say, the cinema or theatre, the clubs provide cheap entertainment. The Internet has played its part as well. Once seen as foreshadowing the end of reading, not only does the Internet allow people even cheaper access to books, but it also acts as a conduit for readers hungry to join a particular reading club. A further draw is the number of people who read for pleasure. With reading being listed as the most popular major leisure activity, according to a survey carried out over a four-week
15 period in 2002 in the UK (65% constant since 1996), there is no shortage of willing participants.

C The clubs vary, ranging from cosy get-togethers in friends' houses, with or without set rules and with or without food and drink, to more formal, official set-ups in educational-cum-literary establishments like libraries, sometimes with literary functions with guest speakers. The overwhelming majority are of a more unthreatening, easy-going nature. People come and go, but the cohesion of the groups seems to live on
20 with new ones springing up to replace those which have faded away.

D From the literary point of view, the focus of each group is different as it depends solely on the make-up of the members and their predilections. There are reading clubs which specialize in football, romance, horror, science fiction and so on. Groups can focus on one type or they can be eclectic, combining different types of fiction like romance with, for example, cricket. Some may even dress up in the style of
25 the characters or the time that a story took place to bring a mystery or an old classic to life. With such a variety of choice, book clubs are sure to survive and expand.

5 Complete the summary below using the comments made by a student to help you.

> **1** .... for most people is a very relaxing **2** .... , which can, however, mean that a lot of time is spent on one's own. Yet, it does have compensations. Reading allows one to **3** .... from the real world, which is not a bad thing these days. There is nothing like losing yourself in a **4** .... , whether it be a serious work like a scientific article, or something like a romantic **5** ....

Technique

Use context and your own knowledge as well as the reading passage to complete summaries. Build up your own picture of the summary as you skim it. This picture building is called 'activating schemata'.

1 I think it's an activity related to books.
2 It's a noun to do with something you do or like.
3 I am sure it's a verb here. The real world is like a prison. So?
4 This one is clear! What are we talking about?
5 This must be another word for a book.

Completing multiple-choice questions

1 Look at the multiple-choice questions. Answer the hint questions next to them.

> **Technique**
>
> Study the structure of multiple-choice questions as you prepare for the exam. Notice the relationship between the stem and the alternatives. Is it a cause and effect relationship? Is it one of action and purpose? Or do the alternatives contain an evaluation of something?

1 The increase in book clubs has occurred mainly because they

    A perform a social function.

    B fulfil an intellectual need.

    C cater for people from a variety of backgrounds.

    D solve the social problems of the participants.

Question 1

a Is the question about reasons or consequences?

b Which word in the question indicates that you should look for the most important option?

2 The number of people who read for pleasure in the UK

    A shows that the Internet has some benefits.

    B means that the cost of books will be kept down.

    C ensures there will always be a pool of readers to supply book clubs.

    D means that cinemas and theatres are losing money.

Question 2

a Are you looking for the cause or the effect of the number of people reading?

b In the passage, what reason is given for the spread of book clubs?

c Which option refers to something not mentioned in the text?

3 Which of the following best describes most book groups mentioned by the writer?

    A restrictive

    B formal

    C small

    D informal

Question 3

a What kind of words are options A–D?

b Which similar words in paragraph C describe the different types of groups?

c Which phrase in paragraph C indicates most of the clubs?

4 Books for discussion in groups are

    A restricted to one type.

    B dependent on member preference.

    C limited to several different authors.

    D dependent on the chairperson's reading list.

Question 4

a Which options describe who chooses the books?

b Which options describe the limitations on book choice?

c Which option here is definitely false and which two are not given?

5 The writer of the article thinks that

    A book clubs have a certain future.

    B book clubs will expand slowly but surely.

    C book clubs may not survive.

    D the variety of book clubs will increase.

> **Question 5**
>
> a Is the question asking about the writer's opinion or the writer's purpose?
>
> b Which option accurately paraphrases this opinion?
>
> c Which wrong option is the opposite of the writer's opinion, and which two are not given?

2 Answer the multiple-choice questions.

Analysing questions

1 To some extent, the language and structure in multiple-choice questions are predictable. Match the lists of language 1–7 which may be found in multiple-choice stems with the correct category from a–g.

a Choose the correct effect/outcome/consequence.

b Choose the cause or reason for something.

c Identify questions relating to qualifying words.

d Identify the purpose of an event or item.

e Identify the best action/tool for a particular purpose.

f Explain what general point a specific example relates to.

g Give the writer's main conclusion/purpose/opinion for the whole text.

1 mainly
usually
the majority
the most

2 … leads to …
… ensures that …
… means that …
… causes …
… resulting in …

3 … is used for …
The main use/purpose of … is to …

4 The writer refers to … to show/ illustrate …
… is an example of …

5 In order to achieve/do something, …

6 … because …
… as a result of …
… is caused by …

7 The writer's conclusion/opinion/purpose is best summarized as …
The writer concludes that …
The writer believes that …
The writer's main point is that …

2 Make a checklist of the language features in True/False/Not Given statements, paragraph and section headings. Use exercise 1 to help you.

> **Technique**
>
> Make a checklist of the features of all question types in the exam such as True/False/Not Given or paragraph and section headings. You can use these checklists for revision purposes. Update the checklists as you notice more features.

Improve your IELTS word skills

1 Divide the following verbs into three groups with similar meanings.

> assess ▪ condemn ▪ disapprove ▪ appraise ▪ censure ▪ endorse ▪ condone
> criticize ▪ appreciate

2 Write the corresponding nouns for the verbs in exercise 1.

3 Choose the most suitable noun from exercise 2 to complete the sentences below.

   a The team carried out a detailed _____ of the risks involved.

   b The professor has published several works of literary _____ .

   c The results of the election are a clear _____ of the government's policies.

   d At the end of the opera, the audience showed their _____ by clapping enthusiastically.

   e In his very critical article, the author expresses his strong _____ of reality TV.

4 Make a noun from each of the following verbs to complete the sentences below.

> judge ▪ perceive ▪ believe ▪ think ▪ analyse ▪ condemn ▪ conceive ▪ discriminate

   a Public _____ of the use of money for arts promotion was very harsh.

   b He carried out an in-depth _____ of the extent of progress in this area.

   c There was obvious _____ in favour of funding for science.

   d We need to reserve _____ until we are in possession of all the facts.

   e The general _____ appears to be that artists are somehow superior to scientists.

   f News about current issues barely affects the public's _____ generally.

   g Some artists seem to have no _____ of the way science is changing our view of the world.

5 Contradict the verbs in italics in each sentence below. In most cases you can do this by adding a prefix to the existing verb.

   Example
   The government *defended* the main arguments advanced. (opposed)

   a The government *undervalued* the contribution made by various people.

   b The effects of lack of light on humans are *understood* by most people.

   c The local residents strongly *approved* of the building of the arts complex.

   d The various publications *praised* the contents of the book.

   e The company *judged* the timing of the film's release for maximum coverage.

   f It is clear that the scientific community *believed* the results of the research.

> **Technique**
>
> When you record a new vocabulary item, check if you can add prefixes or suffixes to it. Write the new item together with any other words you can form from it. This helps you to create 'word families', e.g. approve/disapprove/approval/disapproval.

Reading Passage 7

1 You should spend 20 minutes on questions 1–13, which are based on Reading Passage 7.

Sciart – connections between two cultures

Sciart was originally established to fund 'visual arts projects which involved
an artist and a scientist working in collaboration to research, develop
and produce work which explored contemporary biological and medical
science'. Over time, the programme expanded to cover a wider range of
5   arts and science activity. In total, Sciart supported 118 projects with nearly
£3 million of funding to increase interest and excitement in biomedical
science among adults; to encourage collaborative creative practice between
disciplines in the arts and science; and to create a group of artists looking at
biomedical science and build capacity in this field.

10 Interview evidence from those involved in Sciart projects suggested that the
collaborations between artists and scientists had helped to raise awareness
among project participants and the wider public of connections between aspects of the arts
and of the sciences. An effect of this had been to encourage, at policy making and funding
levels, more interest to be taken and more resources to be devoted to encouraging interactions
15 between the two. As one participant who was interviewed commented:

> *Connecting the sensory with the conceptual is something that is fundamental
> to artistic and scientific method. That awareness has got lost at a public
> level. And Sciart collaborations and the publicly visible outcomes help to
> demonstrate those connections, which have tended to become ignored.*
20 > *Sciart has made the similarities between science and art more evident.*

Interviews with a significant number of artists and scientists who had
participated in Sciart-funded projects revealed that the process of
collaboration and of observing each other's professional practices and
cultures had led to previously unnoticed similarities between the 'two
25 cultures' being recognized. The process of recognition provided a point of
familiarity that generally seemed to encourage or reassure those concerned.
The combination of strangeness and familiarity was perceived by some as a
basis on which to engage in collaboration across disciplines.

Scientists' testimonies:
30 > *It has made me think more about the coming together of art and science. At the centre of
> scientific and artistic thinking there are acts of creativity, and I don't think that those acts
> of creativity necessarily differ, although the content may differ. In designing an experiment,
> a thought will come to you that 'something is worth looking at, and I have to be able to
> recognise what the value is within that'.*

35 > *There are surprising parallels with being a scientist. You spend a lot of time getting funding
> and writing reports, and only a small proportion doing the actual science. Each grant is for
> time-limited funding, so like the artists we are always thinking about where the next funding is
> going to come from.*

Artists' testimonies:
40 > *I was intrigued by the radical differences between the artistic process and the scientific
> method, but also by the overlaps, such as the opening up of new ideas, the creative
> manipulation of materials and the process of experimentation. Both science and art require*

45 *creative thinking in their own ways, and they both require observation of the natural world. As an artist, as well as a scientist, you also need to pay attention to detail. There seems to be a lot in common but also a lot that is very different, and that seemed like a nice basis to form new relationships on …*

The main thing is the similarities not the differences. You spend 75 per cent of your time applying for funding, and 20 per cent writing reports, and just 5 per cent actually doing the work. That is the same in both fields. Also there is that commercial lure in science to make money by working
50 *on cures for things like obesity, which means that if you remain within the academic research you effectively take a pay cut to do that. That is the same in the art world as well.*

It was very clear from the testimonies of interviewees from both sides of the art–science divide, and from those participating in projects as well as those observing them, that a great deal of mutual respect between the 'two cultures' had grown up as a consequence of Sciart-funded collaborations.

55 *I've seen plenty of evidence that artists and scientists now view each other's cultures differently. There is a lot of anecdotal evidence of scientists being astonished by the level of both skill and hard labour that goes into the creation of artwork, and similarly a degree of astonishment amongst the artists about the ability and excitement of scientists in dealing with ideas and with imaginative concepts. So, there was I think a process of mutual eye-opening …   (Scientist)*

60 *A strength is that it has enabled people from both sides of the Sciart divide to gain access to different ways of doing things, and that it has begun to break down some of the prejudices in the two camps.   (Arts expert)*

Technique

1 Survey the whole reading passage and the questions.
2 Skim the title and predict the contents of the passage.
3 Skim the reading passage in no more than two minutes.
4 Skim the questions. Use the questions to help you improve your understanding of the general content of the reading passage

---

Questions 1–6

Complete the summary.

*Choose **NO MORE THAN TWO WORDS** from the passage for each answer.*

Background to the Sciart projects

The Sciart programme was basically launched to encourage **1** .... between scientists and artists, eventually covering 118 projects that were not just involved in art and biomedical science. When participants were interviewed about the Sciart projects, they felt the project increased **2** .... of the connections between the **3** .... and .... among themselves and the general public. The result of this was that attempts were made to increase **4** .... between both cultures. One interview comment was that Sciart had made the **5** .... between science and art **6** ....

Questions 7–10

Classify the following comments about Sciart according to whether they were made by:

A Scientists

B Artists

C Both scientists and artists

7 Detail is important in both art and science.

8 The funding of projects takes up a lot of time.

9 Making money is attractive to both artists and scientists.

10 While the content may be different, the creative process isn't.

Questions 11–13

*Choose the correct letter, **A**, **B**, **C** or **D**.*

11 In both the artistic and scientific fields

    A a majority of the time is devoted to work.

    B only a small amount of time is spent working.

    C funding applications require less time than writing reports.

    D networking takes up a lot of valuable time.

12 The programmes funded by Sciart have resulted in

    A a fall in respect between artists and scientists.

    B government funding for similar collaborative projects.

    C an increase in the divide between artists and scientists.

    D an increase in respect between artists and scientists.

13 The amount of work involved in creating a piece of art

    A made little impression on scientists.

    B made scientists a little surprised.

    C surprised scientists a lot.

    D only impressed imaginative scientists.

Technique

Multiple-choice questions

1 Predict the likely location of the answer in the passage.

2 Predict answers by using what you know from previous questions.

3 Identify the relationship between the options and the stem (e.g. cause and effect).

4 Identify scan words in the stem and use them to locate the correct section.

5 Read around this section and match the meaning in the text with the correct paraphrase from the options.

---

2 Answer these questions.

  a Should more arts than science subjects be taught in schools? Why/Why not?

  b Do you think people should be worried about future developments in science? Should the work of scientists be controlled and restricted by governments? Why/Why not?

  c Do people have the knowledge to understand scientific developments? Why/Why not?

UNIT AIMS

READING SKILLS
Labelling a map
Completing short answer questions
Labelling a diagram (2)
Classifying information

EXAM PRACTICE
Completing a table
Completing short answer questions
Completing multiple-choice questions

Labelling a map

1 Complete each paragraph with the name of the correct civilization and answer the questions below.

Inca   Norse

1 .... mythology provides a typical example of how natural processes are dramatized in early cultures. People believed that Thor, son of the god Odin, rode across the sky in a chariot. When he swung his hammer, it made thunder and lightning, and of course also rain which was necessary for growing crops.

2 The .... mythology personified a number of natural forces, the most important of which was Inti, the sun god. The .... emperors were believed to be descended from him.

a People today often prefer to find scientific rather than divine explanations for natural processes. What have we gained or lost by this?

b What lessons could modern society learn from our ancestors in order to improve our relationship with the environment?

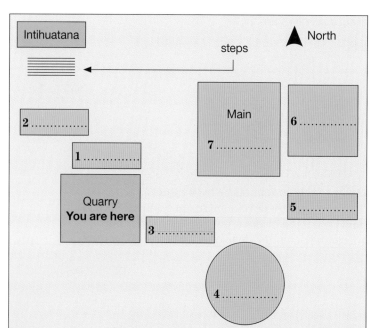

2 Study the map of Machu Picchu. Answer the questions about the map.

a Where is the main reference point for the map?

b What lies north of the Quarry?

c What types of words are missing in each blank space?

d What type of place do you think 7 is?

e How would you describe the location of each place 1–6 in relation to 7?

3 Skim the extract below from an article on the nature reserve around Machu Picchu and label the map in exercise 2.

Nature, gods and man in harmony

Discovered in 1914 by Hiram Bingham with partial backing from The US Geographic Society, Machu Picchu is situated in a natural reserve famed as much for its spectacular flora and fauna as the majesty of its buildings in perfect harmony with its natural surroundings.

The complex stands more than two thousand metres above sea level, 120 kilometres from
5   Cuzco, in Peru. On the terraces above and to the west of the Main Lawn stand three temples. On the left, just north of the Quarry, stands the Temple of the Three Windows. This three-walled structure commands a spectacular view down across the Main Lawn to the mountain peaks in the east. Just north-west of this building is situated the Principal Temple with *Intihuatana* (the Sun's hitching stone) at the top of a flight of steps beyond the Temple. The purpose of this stone was
10 principally astronomical. East of the Lawn and on the same level are the ruins of the Common District where the workers who looked after the complex for the Emperor lived. Other notable locations at Machu Picchu are the Royal Sector, which is situated on the same level as the Main Lawn to the south and just east of the Quarry. Just south of this sector stands the Temple of the Sun, Machu Picchu's only circular building. Inside there is an altar and a trapezoidal window
15 known as the Serpent Window. At the south-east corner of the Main Lawn, just south of the Common District, is the Temple of the Condor, with a prison complex directly behind it.

4 Which of the following techniques do you think are useful to help you label the map?

a   Reading the whole passage first and underlining all the names and directions and then looking at the map.

b   Numbering the names in the text according to the map.

c   Underlining the directions: north, etc.

d   Putting boxes around the names.

e   Trying to complete several items in the map at the same time.

Completing short answer questions

1 Answer the short answer questions about the reading passage on page 63. Use no more than THREE WORDS from the passage for each answer.

 1 What kind of purpose did *Intihuatana* serve? _____

 2 Which area is found on the east side of the Main Lawn?

 _____

 3 What shape is the Temple of the Sun? _____

 4 How many walls does the Temple of the Three Windows have?

 _____

 5 What lies behind the Temple of the Condor? _____

 6 What is the name of the window in the Temple of the Sun?

 _____

2 Complete questions 1–5 about the reading passage on page 63 using no more than TWO WORDS. Then find the correct answers in the passage.

 1 _____ shape is the window in the Temple of the Sun?

 2 _____ did the complex of Machu Picchu belong to?

 3 _____ is the scene across the lawn described?

 4 _____ helped fund Hiram Bingham?

 5 _____ is Machu Picchu from Cuzco?

Labelling a diagram (2)

1 Study the diagram and predict the answers. Use the information in the diagram and your general knowledge.

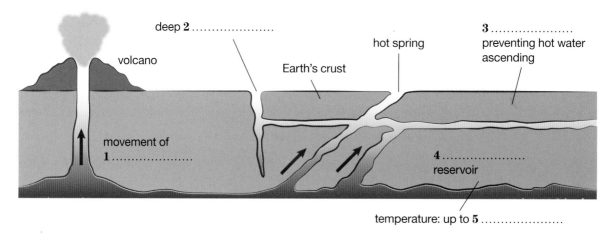

deep **2** ....

3 ....
preventing hot water ascending

volcano

hot spring

Earth's crust

movement of
1 ....

4 ....
reservoir

temperature: up to **5** ....

2 Scan paragraph one in the reading passage on page 65 and using no more than TWO words or a number from the passage, label the diagram.

Geothermal energy

Since heat naturally moves from hotter regions to cooler ones, the heat from the Earth's centre (over 7000° Fahrenheit) flows outwards towards the surface. In this way, it transfers to the next layer of rock or mantle. If the temperature is high enough, some of this mantle rock melts and forms magma. The magma ascends in its turn towards the Earth's crust. At times it forces itself up to the actual
5   surface where it builds volcanoes. More often it remains well below the Earth's crust, creating vast subterranean areas of hot rock. In such regions, there are deep cracks, which allow rainwater to percolate underground. This water is heated by the hot rock to a high temperature. Some of this water travels back up to the Earth's surface where it will appear as a hot spring or a geyser. However, if this ascending hot water reaches a layer of impermeable rock, it remains trapped, forming a geothermal reservoir. Much
10   hotter than surface hot springs, such reservoirs can reach temperatures of 700° Fahrenheit and are a rich source of energy. If geothermal reservoirs are close enough to the surface, they can be reached by drilling wells. Hot water and steam shoot up the wells naturally, and can be used to produce electricity in geothermal power plants. Unlike fossil fuels, geothermal energy produces relatively little greenhouse gas.

A few geothermal power plants depend on dry-steam reservoirs which produce steam but little or no water. In
15   these cases, the steam is piped up directly to provide the power to spin a turbine generator. The first geothermal power plant, constructed at Lardarello in Italy, was of this type, and is still producing electricity today.

Most currently operating geothermal power plants are either 'flash' steam plants or binary plants. Flash plants produce mainly hot water ranging in temperature from 300° to 700° Fahrenheit. This water is passed through one or two separators where, released from the pressure of the underground reservoir,
20   it 'flashes' or explosively boils into steam. Again, the force of this steam provides the energy to spin the turbine and produce electricity. The geothermal water and steam are then re-injected directly back down into the Earth to maintain the volume and pressure of the reservoir. Gradually they will be reheated and can then be used again.

A reservoir with temperatures below 300° Fahrenheit is not hot enough to flash steam but it can still be used to
25   generate electricity in a binary plant. In these plants, the heat of the geothermal water is transferred to a second or binary fluid, such as isopentane, which boils at a lower temperature than water. The steam from this is used to power the turbines. As in the flash steam plant, the geothermal water is recycled back into the reservoir.

Classifying information

1 Using the reading passage above, classify the features in sentences 1–5 according to which type of geothermal plant they characterize.

A dry steam plants	**1** There are examples which are in use today.
B flash steam plants	**2** They use geothermal reservoirs with temperatures over 300° F.
C binary plants	**3** They use steam from the Earth and not water.
D all of them	**4** The vapour which spins the turbines is not produced from water.
	5 They are relatively easy on the environment.

> **Technique**
>
> Locate the different categories or classes in the reading passage and put a box around them. Read the sentences to be classified. Scan the text around the boxed categories to locate the information in the sentences. Note in the IELTS exam the information to be classified may also be in phrases, i.e. noun phrases or clauses.

2 Answer the following questions about the techniques you used in exercise 1.

    a Is it better to scan the passage for the plants or for the features?

    b Is it better to put a box around the plant names and label them A, B, etc. or to underline the words?

    c Is it better to try to answer 1–5 simultaneously or one at a time?

Improve your IELTS word skills

1 Which words in the box mean the same as *feature*?

> article ■ characteristic ■ trait ■ attribute ■ character ■ quality

2 What synonyms do you know for *group*?

3 Match each phrase a–h with a suitable noun 1–8.

a	a make of	**1**	car
b	a species of	**2**	writing
c	a genre of	**3**	horse
d	a class of	**4**	medicine
e	a field of	**5**	study
f	a branch of	**6**	virus
g	a breed of	**7**	mammal
h	a strain of	**8**	animal

4 Which of these words can be used as synonyms of the nouns in exercise 3?

> brand ■ variety ■ sort ■ type

5 Complete the following table with the correct form of the word.

Noun	Verb	Adjective
character	characterize	_____
distinction	distinguish	_____
example	_____	
feature	_____	
illustration	illustrate	illustrative
indication	indicate	_____
type	_____	_____

6 Complete the sentences below using one of the verbs in the box.

> classified ■ differentiated ■ satisfied ■ defined ■ catalogued ■ related

a The library books are _____ meticulously and given a barcode reference.

b Chimpanzees, gorillas and orang-utans are all closely _____ species.

c Several specific criteria must be _____ before any member is included in the group.

d A marsupial can be _____ as any mammal which gives birth to underdeveloped young and rears them in a pouch.

e Fungi may be _____ into three broad groups: yeasts, moulds and others.

f Sometimes members of a subspecies of mammal can only be _____ by experts with specialist knowledge.

> **Technique**
>
> Build a bank of words and phrases that relate to classification. It is a common text feature in IELTS reading passages and questions.

Reading Passage 8

You should spend 20 minutes on questions 1–13, which are based on Reading Passage 8.

The beauty of cats

For most people, a domestic cat is a more or less beautiful, usually affectionate but rarely useful member of the family. However, for the people who breed, show or simply admire them, the pedigree aristocrats of the cat world can easily

5   become an obsession. As yet, there is a very much smaller range in the sizes and shapes of cats compared with dogs, which is not surprising when we consider that dogs have been selectively bred for hundreds, if not thousands, of years to develop physical and temperamental characteristics that can

10 be put to work for man as well as admired. By contrast, all breeding of pedigree cats is for purely aesthetic reasons.

Only a few pedigree cat breeds date back beyond the late nineteenth century, and most have been developed since the 1950s. To achieve acceptance, any new breed must be officially recognized by the national and international organizations of 'cat fanciers' that regulate the breeding and

15 showing of pedigree cats. To date, official recognition has been given worldwide to more than 100 different breeds. A fairly small number of these are what might be called 'natural' breeds, with distinctive characteristics that appeared spontaneously, and then became established in the cat population of a particular country or region. Examples include what is popularly known as the Persian, with its long-haired coat; the Russian Blue, with its plush grey 'double' coat; the Siamese,

20 with its slender body, long, narrow face and distinctive colouring; and the Manx cat, with either no tail (a 'rumpy') or a small stump of a tail (a 'stumpy').

More usually, new pedigree cat breeds are the result of meticulously planned breeding programmes designed to establish or enhance attractive or unusual features occurring in non-pedigree cats. Without the intervention of the cat breeder, many of these features would occur only rarely or

25 would have simply disappeared through natural selection. Even the so-called natural breeds have been considerably modified over the years by professional cat breeders striving to match or improve on the breed 'standard', a detailed description of the various points (length and colour of coat, body and head shape, etc) according to which a particular breed is judged in competition.

The majority of cats, both wild and domestic, have fur that is of short or medium length. Long fur in

30 cats can occur either as the result of a 'one-off' genetic mutation, or through the inheritance of the recessive gene for long hair. Long-haired cats were well-established in Persia (now Iran) and Turkey

long before the ancestors of most modern long-haired show cats were taken to Europe and America towards the end of the nineteenth century. Today's pedigree longhairs of Persian type have a cobby (sturdy and rounded) body, a very luxuriant long coat, short, thick legs, a round head, round face, very short nose and large, round, orange or blue eyes. There are separate show classes for Persians of different colours. Also shown in their own classes are various non-Persian longhairs, including Chinchillas, Himalayans (also called Colourpoint Longhairs) and the Turkish Van.

Short-haired pedigree cats can be divided into three main categories: the British Shorthair, the American Shorthair and the Foreign or Oriental Shorthair. To the uninitiated, British and American Shorthairs appear to be no more than particularly fine examples of the non-pedigree family cat. The reality is that selective breeding programmes have achieved a consistency of conformation and coat characteristics in the different pedigree lines that could never be achieved by chance. Pedigree British Shorthairs have a cobby body, a dense, plush coat of a specified colour, short legs, round head, a somewhat short nose and large round eyes of a designated colour. By comparison, pedigree American Shorthairs have larger and less rounded bodies, slightly longer legs and a less round head with a square muzzle and medium-length nose.

The third main group of pedigree cats are the Foreign or Oriental Shorthairs. Some of these breeds, notably the Siamese, Korat and Burmese, did indeed originate in the East, but today these terms are used to describe any breed, of whatever origin, that displays a range of certain specified physical characteristics. Foreign and Oriental cats have a slim, supple body, a fine, short coat, long legs, a wedge-shaped head, long nose, large, pointed ears and slanting eyes. Finally, also included within the pedigree short-hairs, are various miscellaneous breeds which have been developed to satisfy a perhaps misplaced delight in the unusual. Examples include the Scottish Fold, with its forward-folded ears, the Munchkin, with its short, Dachshund-like legs and the apparently hairless Sphynx.

Questions 1–6

Complete the table below

Choose **NO MORE THAN THREE WORDS** *from the reading passage for each answer.*

Features	Coat	Body	Legs	Head	Nose	Eyes
Persian longhairs	luxuriant and long	cobby	**1**	round	very short	round orange or blue
British shorthairs	dense and plush	**2**	short	round	rather short	large and round, designated colour
American shorthairs	dense and plush	larger and less rounded	slightly longer	less round	**3**	
Foreign shorthairs	**4**	slim and supple	long	**5**	long	**6** ....

Questions 7–11

*Answer the questions below using **NO MORE THAN THREE WORDS** from the passage for each answer.*

7   What name does the writer give to breeds such as the Persian, Russian Blue and Siamese?

8   What is the name given to the description of physical features by which a pedigree cat is judged?

9   In which century were long-haired cats first exported from Persia?

10   What class of cat does the Chinchilla belong to?

11   What remarkable characteristic do Scottish Fold cats have?

Questions 12 and 13

*Choose the correct letters, **A**, **B**, **C** or **D**.*

12   The distinctive features of most pedigree cats are the result of

A   enhancing characteristics that appear naturally in cats from a particular region.

B   using breeding schemes to promote features which are found in non-pedigree cats.

C   genetic changes which occurred spontaneously in some cats in the late nineteenth century.

D   a misplaced pleasure in producing unusual looking cats.

13   The writer's main purpose in this article is

A   to outline the history of breeding pedigree cats.

B   to criticize the practice of producing odd characteristics in cats.

C   to classify the different breeds of pedigree cats.

D   to compare the respective practices of cat and dog breeders.

2   Answer these questions.
   a   Are cats and other animals common pets in your family? Why/Why not?
   b   What other kinds of pets are popular in your country?
   c   What are the benefits of keeping pets for young people? For old people?

Technique

Short answer questions

1 Look for a scan word in each question.

2 Locate where the answers begin and end in the reading passage using the scanning words. Look at the names in questions 7 and 11.

3 In the passage, put a box around all the names from the questions.

4 Number the names in the text according to the question.

5 Read around the names to find the answers. Try to complete several items at the same time.

READING SKILLS
Scanning for meaning
Identifying sentence function
Matching information to paragraphs (2)

EXAM PRACTICE
Matching information to paragraphs
Answering Yes/No/Not Given statements
Completing multiple-choice questions

Scanning for meaning

1 Read the table which gives the average lifespan for humans in different periods of history. Then answer questions a–c.

Period	Average lifespan
Bronze age	18
Classical Greece	28
Medieval England	33
Late nineteenth century	37
Early twentieth century	50
Early twenty-first century	68

a   What reasons can you think of for the increase in lifespan?
b   Some people in Classical Greece lived to a ripe old age. For example, Sophocles, the writer, died at the age of 91. Why do you think the average was so low?
c   What are the disadvantages of the average person living so much longer than in the past?

Technique

Practise scanning for synonyms of words and phrases. Always think of possible synonyms and paraphrases in exam questions. This will also help you build your vocabulary. You can, for example, keep lists of words and structures to reflect cause and effect, e.g. impact, influence, cause, as a result of, etc. Also record words and phrases with examples and practise transforming them into different word types.

2 Look at phrases a–f and think of your own synonyms or phrases with similar meaning. Then match each one with a phrase 1–6.

a   negative consequence
b   non-conventional medicine
c   indispensable part
d   psychological well-being
e   congenial surroundings
f   enormous progress

1   vital role
2   unfortunate outcome
3   good mental health
4   pleasant environment
5   considerable improvement
6   alternative therapy

3 Look at phrases a–e and think of a noun with a similar meaning for each. Then scan paragraph A on page 71 for nouns with a similar meaning and underline them.

a   best period of their life
b   period
c   highest point
d   difficulty
e   benefits

Prime time rules

A People were not that long ago considered as entering their prime at 40. This was the age at which the peak of their wisdom and power was likely to be reached. Not any more. For an increasing number of people, it is now much later, between 50 and 65, which is effectively when people are thinking of retiring. And so, far from being the major problem that has been exercising politicians and individuals in recent years, the increasing numbers of active over fifties with a later and longer prime should be seen as assets to society, economically and socially. Provided, that is, that they are allowed to contribute to the community.

B Anxiety about funding 'older people' in general is based on a view of the over fifties and sixties living a life of decrepitude with costly nursing home care, and being a drain on the country's wealth. Stereotypical images of senior citizens haunt the general population. Perception tests in studies have shown that people who expect the so-called age-related illnesses like deafness and mental decline to happen in their old age conform to the stereotype and fulfil the prophecy. Thus, it is not surprising that negative images permeate society. More positive images of people in their prime or older in the media, etc would be a good start. There are encouraging signs that the boundaries of this stereotype are already being challenged. There are already TV programmes, for example, about people in their seventies and eighties involved in sports like sky-diving more often associated with the young. Some adverts are pushing the boundaries further by using older models to target beauty products at older sections of the population. After all, who has the accumulated wealth?

C Before looking at what, if anything, can be done to make sure that people can enjoy their prime and feel they can make a contribution to society, we should look at the causes of longevity. Technological advances primarily in medical science are often held up as the principal cause. However, education, wealth and the wide range of leisure pursuits available, along with a host of other factors, have led to a marked improvement in living standards throughout the world. People are, as a result, arriving at the threshold of retirement more active, physically and mentally, than any previous generations and in greater numbers, challenging the view that being 50 or even 60 is old.

D And the magic recipe to enhance our prime? It's all very basic stuff and not really magic at all. It does not need government committees or armies of bureaucrats to devise training packages. People are enhancing their 'prime' time without unnecessary interference. Government and planners should seek to inform themselves of what is happening rather than imposing some clumsy 'innovation'. Research has shown that physical exercise causes changes in the structure of the brain. MRI scans on a cohort of patients aged 58 to 77 have shown increases in the substance of the brain itself are brought about by exercise. There is evidence that the areas of the brain involved in memory and attention benefit from exercise – the areas that show the greatest age-related decline in humans.

4 Look at phrases a–e and think of a word or phrase with a similar meaning for each. Then scan paragraphs B–D in the passage for phrases with a similar meaning and underline them.

a a waste of the nation's money
b main factor
c questioning the notion
d secret formula
e introducing an unwanted new measure

5 Think of synonyms for the key words in the sentences below.

a People in general are surrounded by conventional images of old people.
b Makers of beauty products could launch cheaper cosmetics aimed at older people.
c Research indicates that those who expect to be hard of hearing or senile when they grow old actually go on to become so.
d Administrative workers or government bodies have no need to put together guidelines to educate people.
e Studies have revealed that the brain continues to develop well into old age, regardless of how much exercise is taken.

6 Three of the sentences in exercise 5 match sentences in the passage on page 71. Scan to find the three sentences and underline them.

Identifying sentence function

1 Paragraph A on page 71 contains a suggestion made by the author and a sentence with a conditional meaning. Answer questions a–e below. Then scan to find the sentences.

a Are the words *suggestion* and *condition* likely to be in the text?
b Will you scan the passage for meaning or words?
c Which words do you associate with *suggestion*?
d Which words do you associate with a *condition*?
e Is it efficient to read the whole paragraph?

2 Scan the passage to find examples of functions a–e below, using the same techniques as you did for exercise 1.

a a claim (paragraph A)
b a problem (paragraph B)
c a conclusion (paragraph B)
d a recommendation (paragraph B)
e examples (paragraph B)

3 Are the ideas in paragraph C organized around problem and solution, or cause and effect? Which phrases indicate this?

4 Make a checklist of techniques of your own to scan for meaning for revision purposes. Revise the list as you prepare for the IELTS exam.

1	Think of words with the same meaning as those in a question.
2	
3	
4	
5	

Matching information to paragraphs (2)

1 Think of at least three strategies you have used before to match information to paragraphs and note them in your checklist.

2 Scan the previous passage and match phrases 1–5 to paragraphs A–D.

> **1** the fact that skydiving is more often seen as a pursuit for the young
>
> **2** a reference to research on exercise and brain function
>
> **3** the belief that being elderly means being infirm
>
> **4** the reasons why people live longer
>
> **5** the idea that the over fifties can be of use to society

3 Do the phrases 1–5 match whole paragraphs or parts of paragraphs?

4 Paragraphs E–G below in note form are a continuation of the reading passage on page 71. Match phrases 1–5 below with the relevant paragraph E–G.

E The benefits of diet – as well as exercise – healthy diet – avoiding junk perhaps also staves off mental decline – studies in children learning difficulties – so-called Durham trial
5 – fish oil beneficial – effective on sizeable proportion of children – improves attention, etc, so not old wives' tale – sale of foods/ supplements containing Omega 3 increased intelligence attention span – not sure if
10 benefit adults.

F How people can keep mentally active – greater interest now in mental stimulus to combat/slow down dementia – exercises – 'brain food' puzzles like sudoku, chess, crossword puzzles, mental arithmetic, 15 subtracting backwards seven at a time from 1,000 to zero, showering with your eyes closed – some connection with left brain function as opposed to right brain – latter concerned with the creative side. Maybe more 20 research needed: how opening up use of right brain might enhance mental ability.

G A conclusion – irony – general population 30 per cent obese – young people especially – older people now more active – interest in 25 third age long may it continue – older people show young people the way.

> **1** various methods to improve mental ability
>
> **2** the fact that fish oil supplements may not benefit adults
>
> **3** a comparison between older people and less active young people
>
> **4** how diet helps improve mental activity in children
>
> **5** a recommendation that research into right-brain function should be carried out

Improve your IELTS word skills

1 Match the words below with their function from the box.

- **a** Because
- **b** Consequently
- **c** For instance
- **d** Thus
- **e** Moreover
- **f** Yet
- **g** Although
- **h** In order to
- **i** Provided that

> condition ■ concession ■ example ■ additional information ■ conclusion ■ reason
> contrast ■ purpose ■ result

2 Which is the odd one out in the following sequences and why?

- **a** furthermore/in addition/similarly/therefore/also
- **b** meanwhile/but/however/though/even so
- **c** firstly/secondly/finally/at first/first of all
- **d** initially/at the beginning/firstly/at first
- **e** consequently/as a result/subsequently/as a consequence
- **f** recently/some time ago/lately/not long ago/a short time ago
- **g** when/before/once/after/as soon as

3 To help you find your way around a passage, you can look out for linking words and phrases. In the following sentences, find and underline examples of the functions in the box.

Example

Although I agree with the proposed increase in time, it is more important for the course to be updated. (concession)

> result ■ reason ■ condition ■ concession ■ alternative ■ comparison ■ purpose

- **a** Unless more funds are put into the health service soon, people will suffer.
- **b** Because a record number of heart operations were successful, the programme was expanded.
- **c** The funding dried up, which then led to a major crisis at the health clinic.
- **d** More administrative staff could be employed or more nursing posts created.
- **e** The first drug was pronounced safe to use whereas the second caused a number of serious side effects.
- **f** The government opened three new hospitals so that they would be able to meet their targets.
- **g** Although they may need to slow down a little, people continue to benefit from physical exercise well into old age.

Reading Passage 9

You should spend 20 minutes on questions 1–14, which are based on Reading Passage 9.

Professional strangers: medical anthropology in action

A Back in the 1970s, I was an anthropology student sitting in the library doggedly reading books and articles about the social lives of people in Africa, Asia, and the South Pacific. Why doggedly? The
5 scholarly reading matter covered kinship systems, clan alliances, land tenure and farming and political systems. Rarely did the reader of these texts catch a glimpse of the day-to-day lives of the people written about or what it was like to live amongst
10 them. However, some books started with a preface describing how the anthropologist arrived in the distant village or town of study, found somewhere to live, and started engaging with local people. These accounts were often the most interesting part of the
15 book and whetted my flagging appetite for medical anthropological research.

B Since graduating, I have applied my anthropological training to health-related projects across Africa and Asia. Some contracts have lasted two years and some two weeks. The short-term research I have done is sometimes called 'quick and dirty'. 'Quick' means that surveys are carried out and people interviewed in
20 a matter of weeks rather than years; 'dirty' means that the findings are analysed rapidly without too much concern for 'cleaning' the data so that exact percentages can be calculated and any inconsistencies in what people said can be accounted for. Quick and dirty research elicits the voices of the people for whom a development project is intended. The approach provides facts and figures that guide project design, but may not satisfy purist academics.

25 C A lot of books discuss the ethics and methods of research in more detail than in the past. Such accounts of fieldwork contain useful ideas and guidance, usually in the introductory chapters. There are a number of particularly sensitive areas that people interviewed may be reticent about, notably personal finance, sex and illegal activities. Yet, research of sensitive topics with people considered 'hard to reach' can be interesting and rewarding. There are some basic rules and approaches that should keep the researcher,
30 especially in the medical field, safe and the data collection ethical and effective.

D Anybody going to do fieldwork should dress carefully. It is important to try and wear clothes that do not draw attention to yourself. You do not want to be more conspicuous than you need by being more smartly or formally attired than the people you are going to talk to. Equally, it may be inappropriate to copy the dress code of interviewees, as you risk looking ridiculous.

35 E It is always useful to work with local guides or gatekeepers who can help you reach people who are not part of mainstream society. For example, if you want to study the world of illegal drug users it is best to work with an insider. If you already know any drug users, ask one of them to introduce you to other people in his or her network and to vouch for you. Alternatively, you could approach drug or social service agency workers and ask them to make introductions.

40 F When you interview people, it is important that they are not worried about confidentiality. Often people will not tell you anything of great interest unless they receive assurances that you will not reveal their private business or their full names. When you ask sensitive questions, interviewees may want you to answer similar questions in return, so researchers should be prepared to disclose some personal information. It is important that you do not lie about yourself and what you are doing: this is unethical

45 and you risk being caught out and losing credibility.

G Sensitive questions should be asked in a matter-of-fact manner because, if you appear embarrassed, the respondent will also be embarrassed and will 'clam up'. Do not be, or appear to be, judgemental or shocked, no matter what you hear, as the interviewee will sense your reaction and stop talking. In addition, you should not contradict people even if they have said something that you know to be

50 incorrect. You are there to listen and collect data, not to enter into argument or discussion. When the interview is over you can correct any potentially harmful misconceptions that the interviewee holds. But the most important rule to remember is: if you get nervous or scared, leave the situation.

H Recently, I have started saying to colleagues that there are three qualities required in the anthropologist working in 'the field': liking people; respecting people; curiosity about people's lives. If you cultivate

55 these qualities, the tips I have outlined will come naturally to your work.

Technique

1 Survey the whole reading passage and the questions.
2 Skim the title and predict the contents of the passage.
3 Skim the reading passage in no more than two minutes.
4 Skim the questions. Use the questions to help you improve your understanding of the general content of the reading passage.
5 Use the questions to help you think of the text features in the reading passage, e.g. classification.

Questions 1–6

Which paragraph, (A–H) contains the information in 1–6 below?

NB You may use any paragraph more than once.

1   ways to make contacts with interviewees

2   the fact that the interviewer should appear not to react to what the interviewee says

3   how to dress when talking to interviewees

4   how a deep interest in anthropological research commenced

5   the fact that the interviewer should not argue with the interviewee

6   research that is a rough estimate of a situation

Technique

Matching phrases

1 Identify which phrases refer to a part or the whole of a paragraph, where possible.
2 Decide where the information is likely to be: the beginning, middle or end.
3 Scan for the words in the phrases or synonyms of them.

Questions 7–13

Do the following statements agree with the views of the writer in
Reading Passage 9?

Write

> **YES**   *if the statement agrees with the opinion of the writer*
> **NO**   *if the statement contradicts the opinion of the writer*
> **NOT GIVEN** *if it is impossible to say what the writer thinks about this*

7   Accounts of anthropologists arriving in distant villages were frequently more interesting than any other book contents.

8   More research should be carried out in the field.

9   'Quick and dirty' research is necessary for planned development projects.

10 Contacts with people who are on the fringes of society should only be made through local guides or gatekeepers.

11 Researchers should never answer questions about themselves when they are interviewing.

12 It is better for researchers to continue with an interview even if they are frightened.

13 Researchers need to elicit information without making any apparent judgement on it.

Questions 14

*Choose the correct letter, **A**, **B**, **C** or **D**.*

14 Which of the following statements best summarizes the writer's conclusion?

A   Anthropologists who cultivate certain traits will find that good practice becomes instinctive.

B   Anthropologists working in the field will acquire certain interpersonal skills naturally.

C   Anthropologists' acquisition of the advice given depends on the cultivation of a wide range of qualities.

D   Anthropologists working in the field can easily acquire good habits.

2 Answer these questions.
  a Do you think research into people's behaviour is useful? How?
  b Who would benefit most from such research, e.g. medical professionals?
  c Are we too concerned about research into people's behaviour nowadays, e.g. doing surveys about people's eating and exercise habits?

10 The individual and society

READING SKILLS
Dealing with opinion
Answering Yes/No/Not Given statements
(writer's opinion)

EXAM PRACTICE
Completing short answer questions
Completing multiple-choice questions

Dealing with opinion

1 Describe the photos and answer the questions below.

   a Which people are likely to form a group? How do you know?
   b Which person is alone?
   c Which people are probably not part of a group?
   d Is it becoming easier or more difficult to find places to be alone in the modern world? Is privacy becoming impossible to achieve?
   e What factors in the modern world are having an impact on our private lives? Can these developments be stopped?

2 Match statements 1 and 2 with descriptions a and b.
   1 Governments could do more to help vulnerable people in society.
   2 Governments help vulnerable people in society.

   a The statement is reporting a fact.
   b The statement is giving an opinion.

3 Read the pairs of sentences below. Decide which is a fact and which states an opinion.
   1 a The government spent less money last year on vulnerable people in society.
     b Governments should do more to help vulnerable people in society.
   2 a The encroachment of digital control in all people's lives is inevitable.
     b The survey revealed that sales of digital technology are increasing.
   3 a Practical skills in many traditional societies are under threat because technology is making them redundant.
     b The research showed a range of practical skills were practised in ancient Greek society.
   4 a Foolishly, some employees choose not to be a member of a trade union.
     b Some employees choose not to be a member of a trade union.

4 Find examples of structures a–d in the sentences in exercise 3 on page 78.
Why are these structures used in the sentences?

  a a qualifying adverb
  b a qualifying adjective
  c a cause and effect relationship
  d a modal verb

5 Read statements a–g and decide whether they are opinions or not.

  a A minimum of two players are required to play tennis.
  b The results of the social survey are clearly mistaken.
  c Unfortunately, the tendency to seek fame for its own sake seems to be growing in our society.
  d Sports like football, netball, rugby, etc are taught in schools.
  e It would, I feel, be a good idea to make citizenship classes compulsory in schools.
  f If young people engaged in different activities after school, unsociable behaviour would certainly decline.
  g Formal education fails miserably to meet the needs of the business world and society in general.

6 Underline the words in the statements in exercise 5 which show that they are opinions.

  Example
  It is *better* to spend money on social housing *than* new theatres.

Answering Yes/No/Not Given statements (writer's opinion)

1 Statements 1–6 below relate to paragraph A of the reading passage on page 80. For each statement below, decide if it agrees (Yes) or contradicts (No) the writer's opinion. Write 'Not Given' if it is impossible to say what the writer thinks.

> 1 Having more choice is good because it helps the economy to grow.
>
> 2 Making decisions about minor issues is irritating.
>
> 3 People should seek the help of professionals when making a decision which can have adverse consequences.
>
> 4 If people in poor countries had the same range of choices as those in rich countries, their lives would be easier.
>
> 5 Only people in poor countries do not have any real choices.
>
> 6 Advertisers encourage the mistaken idea that more choice is beneficial.

2 To check your answers to the questions in exercise 1, ask yourself the following questions about the passage. Does the writer

  1 mention a reason why having more choice is good?
  2 describe the effect of making decisions about minor issues?
  3 say when people need to consult professionals?
  4 state a comparison between poor and rich countries?
  5 state a restriction about people in poor countries?
  6 give an opinion about what advertisers do?

Unit 10

Spoilt for choice

A Choice, we are given to believe, is a right. In daily life, people have come to expect endless situations about which they are required to make decisions one way or another. In the main,
5 these are just irksome moments at work which demand some extra energy or brainpower, or during lunch breaks like choosing which type of coffee to order or indeed which coffee shop to go to. But sometimes selecting one option as
10 opposed to another can have serious or lifelong repercussions. More complex decision-making is then either avoided, postponed or put into the hands of the army of professionals, lifestyle coaches, lawyers, advisors, and the like, waiting
15 to lighten the emotional burden for a fee. But for a good many people in the world, in rich and poor countries, choice is a luxury, not a right. And for those who think they are exercising their right to make choices, the whole system is
20 merely an illusion, created by companies and advertisers wanting to sell their wares.

B The main impact of endless choice in people's lives is anxiety. Buying something as basic as a coffee pot is not exactly simple. Easy access
25 to a wide range of consumer goods induces a sense of powerlessness, even paralysis, in many people, ending in the shopper giving up and walking away, or just buying an unsuitable item that is not really wanted in order to solve
30 the problem and reduce the unease. Recent surveys in the United Kingdom have shown that a sizeable proportion of electrical goods bought per household are not really needed. The advertisers and the shareholders of the
35 manufacturers are, nonetheless, satisfied.

C It is not just their availability that is the problem, but the speed with which new versions of products come on the market. Advances in design and production mean that new items are almost ready by the time that 40 goods hit the shelves. Products also need to have a short lifespan so that the public can be persuaded to replace them within a short time. The classic example is computers, which are almost obsolete once they are bought. 45 At first, there were only one or two available from a limited number of manufacturers, but now there are many companies all with not only their own excellent products but different versions of the same machine. This makes 50 selection a problem. Gone are the days when one could just walk with ease into a shop and buy one thing; no choice, no anxiety.

D The plethora of choice is not limited to consumer items. With the greater mobility of 55 people around the world, people have more choice about where they want to live and work – a fairly recent phenomenon. In the past, nations migrated across huge swathes of the Earth in search of food, adventure and more hospitable 60 environments. Whole nations crossed continents and changed the face of history. So the mobility of people is nothing new. The creation of nation states and borders effectively slowed this process down. But what is different now is the speed at 65 which migration is happening.

3 Decide why the following statements about the passage are Not Given.

1 Increased choice makes customers more anxious about overspending.

2 It is important for customers to complain when they are dissatisfied with the electrical goods that they buy.

3 More unnecessary goods tend to be bought in the UK than in the rest of Europe.

4 There should be restrictions on the range of products that can be advertised.

4 Read paragraph C and underline the parts of the passage which the following sentences contradict.

> **1** It is a good thing that new products are so widely available.
>
> **2** Products can be kept and used for longer than in the past.
>
> **3** People don't need to replace computers very often nowadays.
>
> **4** There has always been too much choice for the consumer.

5 Read the following pairs of statements. Decide which one agrees with the writer's opinion in paragraph D.

1 a The phenomenon of migration barely changed the course of history.

  b The phenomenon of migration changed the course of history.

2 a People migrated less after the establishment of frontiers between countries.

  b People migrated more after the establishment of frontiers between countries.

3 a Migration is happening more rapidly than in the past due to modern aviation.

  b Migration is happening more rapidly than in the past.

6 A class of students studying for IELTS were asked to choose four more techniques for Yes/No/Not Given tasks. Which four techniques from a–f do you think they added to the list below?

1 Identify cause and effect statements, then scan for this relationship in the passage.

2 Identify qualifying adverbs such as *always* and adjectives such as *important, crucial, well suited.* Then scan the passage for words with similar/opposite meaning.

3 _____

4 _____

5 _____

6 _____

a Check that comparisons in the statements are actually made in the text.

b Try to predict answers before you check the text.

c Look for words that you know in the statements and underline them.

d Check that the statements are in the same order as in the passage.

e Identify modal verbs like *must, should, can, could* and look for similar expressions in the passage.

f Notice phrases such as *It is important, It is easier to, It is possible to,* etc.

Improve your IELTS word skills

1 Decide if the expression in italics means that the item is part of the larger group or an exception to it.

a All members of the board were in agreement, *apart from* Mr Blake.

b Some people, *myself included*, believe that school exams are too easy.

c All of the books were translated into Spanish, *with the exception of* the last.

d Many gifted musicians have come from musical families, and Mozart and Beethoven were *no exception*.

e All societies, *including* technologically advanced ones, retain certain taboos.

f All employees took part in the strike, *save* the director's PA.

g All of the furniture was designed specially, *bar* the lecturer's desk.

h These essays *can be subsumed under* the wider category of existentialist tracts.

2 Write the noun forms of these adjectives.

lonely ■ solitary ■ remote ■ distant ■ isolated ■ secluded

3 Which two of the three adjectives can combine with the given noun to make common collocations?

a *remote/solitary/secluded* area

b *lonely/solitary/distant* existence

c *isolated/remote/distant* past

d *lonely/solitary/secluded* person

e *remote/solitary/isolated* community

4 Complete sentences a–h with the adjectives in exercise 2 above or with a corresponding noun form.

a There is a _____ chance that the hurricane could wipe out the village.

b The new manager was disliked for his cold and _____ manner.

c Unlike wolves, bears are _____ animals and do their hunting alone.

d He experienced feelings of great _____ after the death of his wife.

e There were a few _____ incidents last night but no serious rioting.

f There is a _____ possibility that he has managed to escape the country.

g After their refusal to withdraw their troops from the area, the country was left diplomatically _____ .

h These days, many universities offer _____ learning programmes.

5 Which of the collocations below imply something usual and which imply something unusual?

popular opinion ■ standard formula ■ peculiar idea ■ eccentric behaviour
odd characteristic ■ conventional wisdom ■ orthodox theory ■ deviant personality

6 Think of other adjectives which can collocate with the nouns in exercise 5 to give a similar meaning. You can recombine some of the ones above.

Reading passage 10

1 You should spend 20 minutes on questions 1–13, which are based on Reading Passage 10.

Animal personalities

A Any cat or dog owner will tell you that their pet has an individual personality, different from other people's pets. But recent research has indicated that different types of personalities are found amongst a far wider range of species than was previously supposed, including not only mammals, but also birds and fish.

5 **B** It was formerly believed that if behaviour varied between members of the same species, this was the result of adaption to different circumstances. Different animals within the same species might show different degrees of readiness to explore unknown territory, but this was just a response to the availability of food or potential mates. If an animal was lucky enough to be in a place where food was plentiful, it would not venture far, whereas in a different
10 environment, it would develop a bolder personality. One early piece of research to question this was published by Huntingford in 1976. She noticed that sticklebacks* often displayed the same degree of aggression or sociability towards others in their group at all stages in their life cycle. Such factors as whether they were seeking mates did not affect their behaviour. This seemed to imply that some sticklebacks were more bold and others less so, not because
15 of their circumstances or a predictable stage in their life but because of something more mysterious called 'personality'; they were simply made like that.

C Of course, there can be other reasons besides personality or environment which cause members of the same species to act differently. In the case of ants, individuals follow different developmental paths so that they take on different roles within the colony, such as soldiers or
20 workers. In some species of insects, an individual may even change its function over time, as in bees, some of whom start out as workers and later become food hunters. But these kinds of roles are not the same as personality. They exist within a large social organism so that it runs smoothly. Personality, on the other hand, is not aimed at maintaining any kind of larger whole.

D Personality differences are difficult to explain from an evolutionary point of view. Different
25 traits have both good and bad consequences, so there is no reason why evolution should favour one over another. Bolder individuals do better when it comes to searching for food but they are also more likely to be eaten by a predator. They may have more success in attracting mates but they are also more likely to fight with rivals and be injured.

E The presence of one trait will often go hand in hand with another, creating clusters of traits
30 known in psychology as behavioural syndromes. For example, studies show that in the case
of birds, adventurous individuals are also likely to be less effective at parenting and that their
offspring are less likely to reach maturity, a further instance of how personality traits may work
against the preservation of the species. In one study of sheep by Denis Reale, it was found
that the male animals who showed more aggression reproduced earlier in life whereas the less
35 aggressive ones bred later. At the same time, the first group tended to die at a younger age.
The more docile rams did not start breeding until later, but they generally lived longer, so in
the end they produced the same number of young as their more aggressive peers.

F How exactly these complex syndromes come about is difficult to determine. One theory is that all
personality traits arise from a choice between a small number of fundamental preferences, such as
40 whether an animal tends to seek or avoid risk. It is an open question, too, as to what extent these
choices might be the same for human personalities. The two types of ram as outlined in Reale's
study could be said to reflect two different lifestyles that we also see in humans, something like
'live fast and die young' versus 'slow but sure wins the race'. Certainly the idea that personality is
based on a limited number of basic preferences seems to be supported by many psychologists.
45 It is an interesting possibility that these oppositions may be the same across much of the animal
kingdom, and only vary in the way they manifest themselves.

*stickleback: a type of small fish

Technique

Read the title and skim the reading passage and questions. Remember you can use the
information from the questions to help you predict the content of the reading passage.

Questions 1–5

*Which paragraph, (**A–F**) contains the following information?*

NB *You may use any letter more than once.*

1   Examples of creatures which carry out specific jobs in a social structure

2   A link between personality and average lifespan

3   The claim that one personality trait will imply certain others

4   A reference to the theory that personality traits are the result of differences
in environment

5   Possible dangers associated with boldness as a personality trait

Questions 6–11

*Compete the sentences below. Use **NO MORE THAN TWO WORDS** from the passage for each answer.*

6 Huntingford's study showed that the sticklebacks' personalities remained the same throughout their ....

7 Ants become soldiers or workers as a result of the .... that they take.

8 The roles within an ant colony are aimed at maintaining a complete ....

9 In Reale's study of rams, a tendency to start breeding earlier was linked with greater ....

10 One basic choice in determining personality may involve an animal's attitude to ....

11 It is possible that the same basic preferences create personalities throughout the ....

Questions 12 and 13

*Choose the correct letter, **A**, **B**, **C** or **D**.*

12 According to the writer, a personality trait

    A is usually the result of either good or bad parenting.

    B can work both for and against an animal's chance of survival.

    C can help an animal to live effectively in a large social group.

    D is probably the result of a process of natural selection.

13 Which is the writer's main idea in this text?

    A Animal personality traits develop as a response to their environment.

    B Individual personalities are not found in animals who live in social groups.

    C Animals can have individual personality traits rather like humans do.

    D Individual personality traits are a uniquely human phenomenon.

2 Answer these questions.

  a Do you think personality is mainly the result of your environment or is it mainly something you are born with?

  b Do you enjoy doing personality tests? In what fields of work could personality tests be useful?

Unit 1

Scanning

1

Possible answers

a The main causes are changing climate or poor land management.

b If the causes are man-made, then possibly the situation could be reversed. Irrigation could help in the short term. Measures to combat climate change are probably required in the long term.

c Both. Global as the causes involve global issues such as climate change and the world economy. There may also be local causes such as people cutting down trees for firewood.

d There are environmental consequences such as less farmland or habitable land, and water shortages. There are economic consequences in that it deprives people of their livelihood. There are social consequences such as increased migration to cities.

2

a You can see Sahel because it is a proper noun and therefore written with a capital letter. Anything written with a capital letter is easy to find.

b Desertification is easy to see because it is a longer word and therefore stands out more.

3

The most helpful suggestions are probably a, b and d. Suggestions e and f might also be helpful.

4

marginal (line 5)
steadily crept (line 10)
Botswana (line 15)
increasing population (line 18)
overcultivation (line 20)
plant species (line 27)
management (line 33)

5

a Diagram 3
b Diagram 5
c Diagram 4
d Diagram 2
e Diagram 1

6

transitional (line 5)
unfortunately (line 10)
surveys (line 11)
severe (line 13)
exhausted (line 20)
bind (line 24)
eventually (line 27)
shea (line 35)

7

a occupy (line 7)
b taking place (line 15)
c scarce (line 19)
d entirely (line 27)
e halt (line 31)

8

a prolonged (line 13)
b productive (line 11)
c erosion (line 26)

9

Possible answers

Covering the left-hand side of the paragraph and scanning then covering the right-hand side; using peripheral vision by concentrating on one word and then moving around a paragraph; jumping at random through a paragraph, and so on.

Completing sentences (gapped)

1

1 adjective
2 noun
3 noun
4 noun
5 adjective
6 noun

2

1 semi-arid (line 6)
2 20/twenty years (line 14)
3 increasing population (line 18)
4 plant species (line 27)
5 preventable (line 30)
6 rainfall (line 32)

Answering True/False/Not Given statements

1

Suggested scanning words:

1 Sahara/Sahel – they are easy to find because they have a capital letter.

2 70 per cent, 30 – they are numbers. Also look for the number in words.

3 southern Africa/Sahel – the name has a capital letter.

4 agricultural land use – *agricultural* is a long word.

5 desertification – it is easy to find because it is long.

6 tree cover – use *desertification* in number 5 to help you.

7 tree conservation, sustainable agricultural land use – long phrases are easy to find.

2

1 slowlry northwards
2 just over, over the last 30 years
3 faster, than in the Sahel
4 not
5 minor
6 if, a loss of
7 more … than sustainable agricultural land use

3

1 False
2 Not Given
3 Not Given
4 False
5 Not Given
6 False
7 Not Given

Common features in True/False/Not Given statements include action and purpose, action and method, present perfect for present result, future prediction, obligation and necessity, inclusion (e.g. all, both) and limitation/exclusion (e.g. only).

4

1 The passage does not give a future prediction. We may think this is likely, but it is not in the passage.

2 Again, the passage does not talk about possible future droughts. It only talks about what has happened up to now (note the use of present perfect in paragraph E).

3 The passage only talks about what has been done up to now. The last sentence, which suggests possibilities for the future, does not mention the UNDP.

4 There is no mention of a specific second project.

Improve your IELTS word skills

1
a general nouns which need a context for their meaning

2
a impact/effect
b changes
c effect
d consequences
e cause
f results
g factor
h role

3
a far-reaching consequences
b dramatic changes
c Gradual development
d profound effect
e favourable outcome
f underlying cause
g limited impact

4
a same meaning
b opposite meaning
c same meaning
d opposite meaning
e same meaning

Reading passage 1

Questions 1–6
1 False
2 True
3 False
4 True
5 Not Given
6 True

Questions 7–12
7 (complete) mystery (line 43)
8 (random) guess (line 55)
9 unanswered questions (lines 60–61)
10 same nest (line 77)
11 stars (line 81)
12 local landmarks (line 85)

Questions 13 and 14
A, E

Unit 2

Skimming

1
a Forbidden City, Beijing; St. Basil's Cathedral, Moscow; Petra, Jordan
b Students' own answers.
c Students' own answers.
d Students' own answers.

2 a

3
a 4
b 5
c List 1 relates to architecture/ building; list 2 relates to travelling by train; list 3 relates to history.
d 1–4 contain nouns and verbs; 5 contains an adjective, a conjunction, prepositions, and pronouns, but no nouns or verbs.

4
The words, which are all associated with engineering, are *construction*, *bridges*, *engineers*, *industrial*, *projects*, and *railway*.

5
The words associated with engineering are *construction engineers*, *Industrial Revolution*, *engineers*, *shipping*, *bridge-building*, *railway construction*, *projects* and *works*.

6
1 C; the words which help are *design competition*, *original judge of the competition*, *rejected all entries to the competition*, *second contest*.
2 A; the words which help are given in the answer to 5 above, and the phrase *challenged and motivated his colleagues* relates to the word *inspiring*.
3 B; the words which help are *Thames Tunnel*, *bore under the Thames*, *river broke through into the tunnel*, *second breach*.

Answering True/False/Not Given Statements

1
1 less important … than
2 less involved ... than
6 at the same age as
7 more difficult than

2
1 False
2 Not Given
3 False
4 False
5 False
6 Not Given
7 Not Given

3
1 Change *less* to more.
2 Remove the words *less … than other engineering fields*.
3 Remove the word *only*.

4
a Not Given
b False
c True

5
1 Not Given
2 Not Given
3 False

Completing sentences (matching endings)

1
2 and 4

2
Endings C and G indicate effects.
Questions
B Who was an important civil engineer?
C What meant the completion of the bridge was delayed?
D What is a symbol of Bristol?
E What was recommenced as a suitable memorial to Brunel?
F What/who was chosen in the second competition?
G What led to a second contest to design the bridge?
H What symbolizes Sydney?

3
1 B
2 G
3 F
4 C
5 A
6 E
7 D

4
Statements a–e are wrong. The correct sentences are:
a Many historical sites worldwide/ are being destroyed by visitors. The word *rewritten* does not collocate with *sites*. The word *sites* collocates with *destroyed*.

b Many old films/are being restored and digitally mastered. The words *films* and *conducted* do not collocate. The words *films* and *restored* and *digitally mastered* collocate.

c Archaeological digs/are rarely conducted for a long period of time. The words *digs* and *known for their breadth of knowledge* do not collocate. The words *digs* and *conducted* collocate.

d Samuel Johnson and Leonardo da Vinci/were known for their breadth of knowledge. The names Samuel Johnson and Leonardo da Vinci do not collocate with *destroyed/visitors*, but they collocate with *known*.

e Past events/are often rewritten by historians. The words *past events* do not collocate with *restored* and *digitally mastered*. The words *events* and *rewritten* collocate.

Improve your IELTS word skills

1
a 1921   b 1891   c 1803   d 1854
e 1952   f 2001   g 1798

2
the early decades of the 1800s, in the early 1800s, the early 20th century, in the mid 19th century

3
a 3 b 5 c 1 d 6 e 2
f 4 g 7

4
b (successful)
c (unsuccessful)

5
1 A   2 B   3 B   4 A   5 B
6 A   7 B   8 A   9 A   10 B

Reading Passage 2

1

Questions 1–7
1 C   2 H   3 F   4 G   5 D   6 B
7 A

Questions 8–11
8 C   9 A   10 B   11 C

Questions 12–14
12 True
13 Not given
14 False

2
Students' own answers.

Unit 3

Labelling a diagram (1)

1
The movement of people/development of agriculture/trade; the development of agriculture and how people eat; the settling of people in cities; the growth of industries/cities.

2

Possible answers
a *Wood* has been used for fuel for cooking, etc. for centuries. *Wind* has been used to generate power in windmills for grinding grain. Now, the energy of the wind is being harnessed to provide energy through wind farms. *Water* has been used to drive mills for grinding corn and for generating electricity. Energy from waves, rivers and the tides of the seas are now being harnessed. *Nuclear* energy is used to provide electricity and for transportation. *Coal* has been used for centuries to provide energy for domestic and industrial purposes. *Human power* has been used for tasks such as building, and pulling, pushing, and carrying. *Animals* have been used for millennia for pulling and carrying goods and for human transport. *Gas* has been used for lighting and cooking. *Oil* has been used for transport and the production of electricity for domestic and industrial purposes.
b Students' own answers.
c Students' own answers.

3
a The diagram shows an early steam engine.
b All the missing words are nouns.

4
1 boiler   2 steam
3 piston 4 cylinder
5 first valve 6 second valve
7 cold water   8 cistern

5
the use of the engine
the source of the power
the effect of the power
and following actions

6
a It was originally used to pump water from mines.
b generated steam, which drove the piston
c When the steam built up, the pressure opened a valve; when the piston reached the top of the cylinder, the first valve was closed
d sprayed cold water….condensing the steam and creating a vacuum
e thus pulling the rod down with it

7
a True
b True
c False
d False
e True
f False
g True

8
spray – aerosol spray; it is used to spray gases such as deodorant
wash – washing machine; it is used to wash clothes
blow – air conditioning unit; it is used to blow cool (or hot) air
vacuum – vacuum cleaner; it is used to vacuum floors
rotate – photocopier, vacuum cleaner; it is used to rotate the sheets of paper/brushes
clean – washing machine, vacuum cleaner; it is used to clean clothes/clean surfaces
cool – air conditioning unit; it is used to cool a room down
copy – photocopier; it is used to make copies of documents
show – television; it is used to show films and documentaries
toast – toaster; it is used to toast bread

9

Possible answers
battery – torch
axle – car
blade – propeller
handle – door
lens – camera
turbine – engine
switch – light

10
Students' own answers.

Completing tables

1

Advantage
benefit
upside
plus

Disadvantage
downside
drawback
stumbling block
problem
handicap

2
The text includes:
benefit (line 2)
downsides (line 4)
strength (line 8)
problem (line 13)
stumbling block (line 15)
drawback (line 21, 32)

3
Students' own predictions.

4
1 public health
2 methane
3 rosy
4 commercial outlets
5 new dawn
6 readily available
7 bright

5
1 Location
2 Types of power
3 Environmental impact
4 Homes supplied

6
method: strategy, technique
means, way, approach, manner
types: kinds, sorts, classes, groups
category, nature, brand, style
impact: consequence, result,
effect, outcome, upshot,
impression, product

7

Possible answer
The table shows which types of
power are available at different
locations, e.g. mouth of the river. The
environmental impact of these types
of power shows wave power has
a high impact while tidal and wind
power have a low impact. In terms
of homes supplied, wind power is
top, with sufficient energy for 31,000
homes. Wave power comes second
with 26,000 homes supplied with
power while tidal energy has the
lowest energy output with 15,000
homes provided for. This amounts to
around 50% less than wind power.

Completing flow charts

1
thirdly – stage three
after that – any stage
subsequently – any stage
simultaneously – no stage
finally – stage four
at first – no stage
in the next phase – any stage
following that – any stage

2
Students' own answers.

3
1 corn
2 distillery
3 fermentation
4 filtration
5 distillation
6 fuel-ethanol plant
7 blending
8 storage
9 distribution

4
a Diamonds formed deep below
  Earth's surface.
b Filtration followed by fermentation.
c Heat generated by buried waste.
d Electricity generated by rotating
  blades.
e Recording published, sold and
  played on radio.

Improve your IELTS word skills

1
1 to extract	12 lays
2 is filtered	13 emerge
3 reacts	14 grow/live
4 is blended	15 grow/live
5 is stored	16 becomes
6 is distributed	17 emerges
7 falls	18 is heated
8 is carried	19 is cooled
9 to fix	20 are destroyed
10 to grow	21 gains
11 are spread	

2
The first and fourth text describe a
production process. Titles:
'The production process for
margarine', 'How bacteria are
removed from milk'.
The second and third texts describe
a life cycle. Titles: 'The life cycle of a
tree', 'The life cycle of a mosquito'.

3
1 extraction		7 fall
2 filtration		8 carrying
3 reaction		9 fixing
4 blending		10 growth
5 storage		11 spread
6 distribution		

Reading Passage 3

Questions 1–7
1 (yellowish powdery) lesions
2 (green) shoots
3 (green) coffee
4 leaves
5 bare
6 defoliation
7 nodes

Questions 8 and 9
8 B   9 A

Questions 10–14
10 C   11 E   12 G   13 B   14 A

2
Students' own answers.

3
Students' own answers.

Unit 4

Predicting

1

Possible answers
a Picture one shows students
  learning as a class as they listen to
  a lecture and picture two shows a
  student receiving individual tuition.
  Students can also learn in small
  groups in tutorials or take part in
  seminars. They can also learn by
  living with families or by video-
  conferencing or over the Internet
  by distance learning.
b Students' own answers.
c Students' own answers.

Possible answer
d Learning is becoming more
  sophisticated as technology
  slowly moves into the classroom.
  For example, computers are
  now common in some parts
  of the world, as are electronic
  whiteboards.
e Students' own answers.

2
a problem
b reasons
c prediction
d types (and reasons)

3

The sequence is iv, i, iii, ii.

4

a iv

b ii and iii

c i – the heading is stating a general idea for the first time

d i relates to a general issue

5

b

6

Students' own answers.

7

Students' own answers.

Answering Yes/No/Not Given (writer's claims) statements

1

a 1, 5 and 7

b 2, 4, 5 and 6

c 2 unnecessary; 3 boring; 4 reluctance; 6 lost; 7 less interested

d The title tells you the writer is defending British people. Statements 2 and 4 are good arguments for this, but you need to check the answer in the passage. Statement 3 appears not to fit with the title. Students make their own predictions here.

2

1 Yes   2 Yes   3 Not Given   4 Yes
5 Not Given   6 No   7 Not Given

3

Students' own answers.

Matching headings (1)

1

Doctor, table and skyscraper are the odd nouns out. You can picture these three words in your head. The other nouns are more general and often require an adjective, noun or a prepositional phrase or a context to give them meaning, e.g. the impact of a university education, Internet problems.

2

1 D   2 C   3 B   4 A

3

1 a   2 d   3 c 4 f

4

These are all very important, but the most important is b.

5

1 b   2 b   3 a

Improve your IELTS word skills

1

unambitious

unconscious

inaccurate

illiterate

immortal

irreplaceable

irrelevant

dissimilar

dissatisfied

asymmetrical

apolitical

2

a irreplaceable

b unconscious

c irrelevant

d dissimilar

e inaccurate

f apolitical

g immortal

h illiterate

I asymmetrical

3

a spelt wrongly

b not funded enough

c nationalization to be put into reverse

d fishing too much

e sit the exam again

f live longer than

g the level it was before the war

h in favour of democracy

i reducing aggression

j after the crisis

k cannot be used

Reading Passage 4

1

Questions 1–7

1 vii   2 i   3 vi   4 iv   5 ix
6 xiii   7 v

Questions 8–10

8 Yes   9 Not Given   10 No

Questions 11–13

11 C   12 B   13 D

2

Students' own answers.

Unit 5

Completing summaries with wordlists

1

Possible answer

a A younger person teaching older people how to use a computer

b Younger people appear to be much faster using new technology. Older people can use it easily as well. It may just be a question of interest.

c Students' own answers.

d Students' own answers.

2

We can predict that the passage is about young people and possibly the fact that too much is expected of them by other people – parents, schools, employers.

3

a The word *report* helps to find the beginning. The words *family members* and *studies and work* help to locate the end.

b The beginning of the summary is the start of the passage. The end is the first sentence of paragraph 4.

4

It is possible to predict the meaning of most words, even if you cannot predict the words themselves, by using the information in the summary and the collocation of words. For example, in 1, the words *wasting* and *time* help you. In 3 and 4, the answers are at the end of the same sentence. In 7, it is clear by now whether the answer is positive or negative.

5

1 L (significant amounts)

2 A (in sequence)

3 I (electronic gizmos)

4 E (messages)

5 J (behaviour)

6 B (revolution)

7 H (negative impact)

6

Students' own answers.

7

1 a considerable amount of … time [line 3]
2 one after the other [line 6]
3 electronic devices [line 7]
4 sending out emails to their friends [line 9]
5 multi-tasking [line 12]
6 ever larger number of electronic devices/electronic wizardry [line 7/16]
7 seriously affecting [line 16]

8

Possible answer

Read the gapped paragraph or sentences before you look at the text.
Use the grammar to decide what kind of word is missing.
If it is a noun, use the presence or absence of the article to decide what kind of noun it could be.
Use the meaning to predict what the word might be.
If the words are given to you in a box, try to narrow it down to two or three possibilities only for each gap.
Scan the reading passage to identify which section the gapped paragraph or sentences refer to.
Read that section carefully, choosing the answers as you go through. The information will be in largely the same order.
At the end, read your completed answer again to check it makes sense.
Check that your answers are missing information and you have not just repeated an idea that is already there in the sentence.

Selecting statements from a list

1

a The statements are probably found after the end of the summary.
b Treat this like a multiple-choice question. We might expect A or D to be true from the point of view of students. We might expect B to be true from the point of view of academics. We might expect F or G to be true from the point of view of employers.

c A *electronic gadgets*; B *multi-tasking/electronic gadgets*; C *study skills*; D *most young people/electronic gadgets*; E *computer use/school*; F *electronic gadgets/capacity to perform/work*; G *overuse/computers/definitely*. *Electronic gadgets* is a long phrase which should be easy to scan for, but, since it comes up often, other scan words are needed.

2

B, D, F

Answering global multiple-choice questions

1

a The word *concludes* suggests the answer is at the end.
b The writer is against the pressure on young people.
c Statement A is a specific criticism mentioned earlier in the text, so can be eliminated.

2

B

Improve your IELTS word skills

1

-al and –ic form adjectives
-ion, -ment and –ing form nouns

2

global, cultural, economic, exception, innovation, distribution, combinations, development, travelling, marketing, positioning

3

action
detection
fulfilment
training
competition
production
settlement

4

strategic
energetic
democratic
habitual
beneficial
influential

5

courageous – adjective
denial – noun
priceless – adjective
useful – adjective
survival – noun
wonderful – adjective
worthless – adjective

6

1 awareness
2 contribution
3 advertising
4 stereotypical
5 attractive
6 friendship
7 proposal
8 loneliness
9 financial
10 discrimination

Reading Passage 5

Questions 1–7

1

1 C developments
2 E crucial force
3 A transformation
4 I role
5 M integration
6 J network
7 O youth travel

Questions 8–10
8–10 A, D and G

Questions 11–13
11 B   12 C   13 D

2
Students' own answers.

Unit 6

Using general nouns

1

Possible answers
a carnival/festival and work culture
b Students' own answers.
c Students' own answers.

2
advantage – benefit
aim – purpose
consequence – outcome
difference – discrepancy
difficulty – problem
factor – influence
hazard – risk

3
a role
b problem
c strategies
d Reservations
e Action
f outline

4

Students' own answers.

Matching headings (2)

1

a Different definitions of culture and research into it.
b i interpretations
ii problem
iii definition
iv no organizing words used
v reason
vi discrepancy
c ii
d It indicates that this heading matches a paragraph containing more than one main idea.

2

Paragraph A ii
Paragraph B iii
Paragraph C i
Paragraph D v
Heading iv appears in paragraph B but it is not developed. It is really a lead-in to paragraph C. Heading vi appears in paragraph C, but it is not the topic of the whole paragraph. It is only there as further evidence that the meaning of cultural behaviour can be difficult to investigate.

3

The plan relates to Paragraph C.
Example 1: ... such as Max Weber ... culture as consisting of systems of shared meaning
Example 2: Claude Levi-Strauss ... culture as a product of the implicit beliefs which underlie it
Example 3: Chris Argyris and Donald Schon ... what people say to explain their cultural behaviour and what really drives this behaviour are often widely different. [...] The search for meaning can therefore be a long and painstaking process, involving long periods of observation and interviews in order to build possible theories.

Matching information to paragraphs (1)

1

1 idea   2 fact   3 fact   4 ways
Phrase 4 is most likely to refer to a whole paragraph as it does not just refer to one fact or idea but compares different ideas.

2

1 B   2 A   3 C   4 C

3

a ways
b Method 1: studying what can be observed
Method 2: asking what beliefs cause this observed behaviour
Method 3: assessing both the other culture and our own

4

i whole (the phrase refers to various strategies, not just one)
ii part
iii part

Matching information to names

1

Margaret Mead (line 19), Max Weber (line 27), Claude Levi-Strauss (line 31), Chris Argyris and Donald Schon (lines 39–40)

2

1 A   2 D   3 B   4 C

Improve your IELTS word skills

1

link, relationship, association

2

Possible answers

How body language and environment are linked/related/associated.

3

1 aim, goal, objective
2 analysis, explanation, interpretation
3 characteristic, feature
4 consequence, effect, outcome
5 difficulty, obstacle, problem

4

Possible answers

a The outcome of the research on stem cells
b A process of producing hydrogen from water for energy
c The link between culture and wealth
d Factors involved in the production of a film
e The part played by the United Nations in protecting cultures under threat

5

Possible answers

a result/consequence
b way/method/procedure
c relationship/connection/correlation/association
d elements/steps
e the role of/contribution of

6

Possible answers

1 The benefit(s) of studying abroad
2 The aim of choosing a particular field of study
3 The problems of studying in another language
4 Ways to study efficiently
5 Examples of good lectures
6 Factors behind choosing a university/field of study
7 The effect of working hard at university

Reading passage 6

1

Questions 1–4

1 vii   2 i   3 v   4 ix

Questions 5–9

5 D   6 B   7 E   8 C   9 A

Questions 10–12

C, D, F

Question 13

13 C

2

Students' own answers.

Unit 7

Completing summaries without wordlists

1

Students' own answers.

2

a Students' own answers.
b Students' own answers.
c Students' own answers.

Possible answer

d Books don't seem to be going out of fashion, even though there are different media for reading, like ebooks and books that can be downloaded onto iPods.

3

Techniques a, c, e and g are all good techniques.

4

1 social
2 relaxed
3 cheap
4 focus
5 eclectic
6 constant
7 expand

5

Possible answers

1 Reading
2 hobby/pastime
3 escape
4 book
5 novel

Completing multiple-choice questions

1

Question 1
a reasons
b *mainly*

Question 2
a effect
b the low cost of books
c D: cinemas and theatres losing money is not mentioned

Question 3
a adjectives
b cosy, formal, official, unthreatening, easy-going
c *The overwhelming majority*

Question 4
a B and D
b A, C and D
c A is false. C and D are not given.

Question 5
a the writer's opinion
b A
c C is the opposite. B and D are not given.

2
1 A
2 C
3 D
4 B
5 A

Analysing questions

1
1 c
2 a
3 d
4 f
5 e
6 b
7 g

2
Students' own answers.

Improve your IELTS word skills

1

assess, appraise
condemn, disapprove, censure, criticize
endorse, appreciate, condone

2
assessment
condemnation
disapproval
appraisal
censure
endorsement
condoning
criticism
appreciation

3
a assessment
b criticism
c endorsement
d appreciation
e condemnation

4
a condemnation
b analysis
c discrimination
d judgement
e belief/perception
f perception/thinking
g concept

5
a valued/overvalued
b misunderstood
c disapproved
d condemned/disapproved of
e misjudged
f disbelieved

Reading Passage 7

Questions 1–6

1
1 collaboration
2 awareness
3 arts, sciences
4 interactions
5 similarities/connections
6 more evident

Questions 7–10
7 B   8 C   9 B   10 A

Questions 11–13
11 B   12 D   13 C

2
Students' own answers.

Unit 8

Labelling a map

1
1 Norse
2 Inca

Possible answers
a We have gained many scientific benefits for the human race as we look for the answer to natural phenomena like the movement of the stars and the Earth. However, we have also lost something, because scientific explanations can take away the mystery from our lives.
b In many respects, our ancestors treated the environment better. They tried not to disturb the balance between the human race and nature. We could therefore learn to only take what we need from the environment, e.g. planting more trees if we cut trees down.

2
a The Quarry
b Two places to be named (1 and 2), then some steps and *Intihuatana*.
c Names of places.
d Some kind of open space or large building.
e 1 and 2 are west of 7;
   3 and 4 are south of 7;
   5 is south-east of 7;
   6 is east of 7.

3
1 Temple of the Three Windows
2 Principal Temple
3 Royal Sector
4 Temple of the Sun
5 Temple of the Condor
6 Common District
7 Lawn

4
The most useful are: b, c and d.

Completing short answer questions

1
1 (principally) astronomical
2 the Common District
3 circular
4 three
5 a prison complex
6 the Serpent Window

2

1 What ...? Trapezoidal
2 Who ...? The Emperor
3 How ...? spectacular
4 Who/Which organization ... ?
  The US Geographic Society
5 How far ...? 120 kilometres

Labelling a diagram (2)

1

Students' own answers

2

1 magma
2 cracks
3 impermeable rock
4 underground/geothermal
5 700 °/degrees Fahrenheit

Classifying information

1

1 D   2 B   3 A   4 C   5 D

2

a The plants.
b Put a box around the plant names
  and then underline the features.
c One at a time is better.

Improve your IELTS word skills

1

characteristic
trait
attribute
quality

2

Possible answers
category
class
sort
grouping
type
kind
subdivision

3

a 1   b 8   c 2   d 7   e 4 and 5
f 4   g 3   h 6

4

brand can replace *make*;
variety can replace *genre*;
sort and *type* can replace all.

5

characteristic
distinctive
exemplify
feature
indicative
typify, typical

6

a catalogued
b related
c satisfied
d defined
e classified
f differentiated

Reading Passage 8

Questions 1–6

1

1 short, thick
2 cobby
3 medium-length
4 fine, short
5 wedge-shaped
6 slanting

Questions 7–11

7 natural
8 the breed 'standard'
9 the nineteenth century
10 non-Persian longhairs
11 forward-folded ears

Questions 12 and 13

12 B   13 C

2

Students' own answers.

Unit 9

Scanning for meaning

1

Possible answers

a There are several reasons; for
  example, advances in medicine,
  better sanitation, improved living
  standards and greater wealth.
b The number of deaths in childbirth
  was probably very high, as was
  the mortality from plagues and
  diseases. Another reason is the
  lack of medicines like vaccines
  available for illnesses like measles
  which are no longer life-threatening
  if prevented.
c There are several disadvantages.
  If an elderly person is chronically
  ill, it can affect their quality of life.
  Moreover, it can cost the family
  and the country more to look after
  someone.

2

a disappointing result
b unorthodox treatment
c key figure
d mental fitness
e attractive setting
f significant development
a 2   b 6   c 1   d 3   e 4   f 5

3

Possible answers
a peak/pinnacle
b time
c zenith
d crisis
e advantages

Answers from the passage
a prime (line 2)
b age (line 2)
c peak (line 3)
d problem (line 8)
e assets (line 12)

4

Possible answers
a a misuse of a country's budget
b major reason
c querying the idea
d hidden method
e bringing in an unwelcome new
  development

Answers from the passage
a a drain on the country's wealth
  (lines 18–19)
b principal cause (line 45)
c challenging the view (line 53)
d magic recipe (line 55)
e imposing some clumsy 'innovation'
  (line 63)

5

Possible answers
a conventional images: typical/
  stereotypical portraits/portrayals
  old people: senior citizens, the
  elderly
b beauty products: cosmetics,
  older people: senior citizens,
  the elderly
c hard of hearing: deaf,
  senile: suffering from dementia
d administrative workers:
  bureaucrats
  government bodies: committees,
  think tanks,
e brain: mind
  old age: advanced years
  exercise: physical activity

6

a Stereotypical images of senior
  citizens haunt the general
  population. (lines 19–20)
c Perception tests in studies have
  shown that people who expect the
  so-called age-related illnesses like
  deafness and mental decline to
  happen in their old age conform
  to the stereotype and fulfil the
  prophecy. (lines 20–25)

d It does not need government committees or armies of bureaucrats to devise training packages. (lines 57–59)

Identifying sentence function

1

a No, it is unlikely.

b meaning

c Words like *measure*, *proposal*, *recommendation* or modal structures like *should* or *could*, *is/would be a good idea*.

d Words like *if*, *if not*, *unless*, *as long as*, *providing*, *provided that*.

e No. Try to look for words that indicate the meaning and read around them. (suggestion: lines 7–13, condition: line 13–14)

2

a For an increasing number of people, it is now much later, between 50 and 65, which is effectively when people are thinking of retiring. (lines 4–7)

b Stereotypical images of senior citizens haunt the general population. (lines 19–20)

c Thus, it is not surprising that negative images permeate society. (lines 25–26)

d More positive images of people in their prime or older in the media, etc would be a good start. (lines 26–29)

e There are already TV programmes, for example, about people in their seventies and eighties involved in sports like sky-diving more often associated with the young. (lines 31–34)

(lines 34 –37) Some adverts are pushing the boundaries further by using older models to target beauty products at older sections of the population. After all, who has the accumulated wealth?

3

The ideas are organized around cause and effect. The phrases from the passage which indicate this are: *make sure that*, *the causes of*, *the principal cause*, *factors*, *have led to* and *as a result*.

4

Students' own answers.

Matching information to paragraphs (2)

1

Students' own answers.

2

1 B   2 D   3 B   4 C   5 A

3

1–3 refer to parts of paragraphs, whereas 4 and 5 refer to whole paragraphs.

4

1 F   2 E   3 G   4 E   5 F

Improve your IELTS word skills

1

a reason

b result

c example

d conclusion

e additional information

f contrast

g concession

h purpose

i condition

2

a *therefore* indicates result, whereas the others indicate additional information

b *meanwhile* indicates at the same time, whereas the others indicate contrast

c *at first* relates to time, whereas the others relate to numerical sequence

d *firstly* relates to numerical sequence, whereas the others relate to time

e *subsequently* relates to time, whereas the others relate to result

f *some time ago* indicates distant time, whereas the others indicate recent time

g *before* indicates earlier than when, whereas the others all relate to the time when

3

a Condition: <u>Unless</u> more funds are put into the health service soon …

b Reason: <u>Because</u> a record number of heart operations were successful …

c Result: <u>which then led</u> to a major crisis at the health clinic …

d Alternative: More administrative staff could be employed <u>or</u> more nursing posts created.

e Comparison: <u>whereas</u> the second caused a number of serious side effects.

f Purpose: <u>so that</u> they would be able to meet their targets.

g Concession: <u>Although</u> they may need …

Reading passage 9

1

Questions 1–6

1 E   2 G   3 D   4 A   5 G   6 B

Questions 7–13

7 Yes   8 Not Given   9 Not Given
10 No   11 No   12 No   13 Yes

Question 14

14 A

2

Students' own answers.

Unit 10

1

Possible answers

a The schoolchildren

b The mountain walker

c The people on the boat

d Students' own answers

e Students' own answers

2

1 b   2 a

3

1 a fact b opinion

2 a opinion b fact

3 a opinion b fact

4 a opinion b fact

4

a *Foolishly* in 4a

b *inevitable* in 2a

c *because* in 3a

d *should* in 1b

The words are used to indicate the writer's opinion.

5

a not an opinion

b an opinion

c an opinion

d not an opinion

e an opinion

f an opinion

g an opinion

6

b *clearly mistaken*

c *Unfortunately*

e *It would, I feel, be a good idea.*

f *If … , would certainly decline.*

g *fails miserably*

Answering Yes/No/Not Given statements (writer's opinion)

1

1 Not Given
2 Yes
3 Not Given
4 Not Given
5 No
6 Yes

2

1 No   2 Yes   3 No   4 No   5 No
6 Yes

3

1 There is no mention of overspending.
2 The passage doesn't mention whether they are dissatisfied or not.
3 There is no comparison between Europe and the UK. Only the UK is mentioned.
4 The writer does not suggest that restrictions should be placed.

4

1 It is not just their availability that is the problem …
2 Products also need to have a short lifespan so that the public can be persuaded to replace them within a short time.
3 Products also need to have a short lifespan so that the public can be persuaded to replace them within a short time. The classic example is computers, which are almost obsolete once they are bought.
4 Gone are the days when one could just walk with ease into a shop and buy one thing; no choice, no anxiety.

5

1 b   2 a   3 b

6

a, b, e and f

Improve your IELTS word skills

1

a exception
b part
c exception
d part
e part
f exception
g exception
h part

2

loneliness
solitude
remoteness
distance
isolation
seclusion

3

a remote/secluded
b lonely/solitary
c remote/distant
d lonely/solitary
e remote/isolated

4

a remote
b distant
c solitary
d loneliness
e isolated
f remote
g isolated
h distance

5

Usual
popular opinion
standard formula
conventional wisdom
orthodox theory

Unusual
peculiar idea
eccentric behaviour
odd characteristic
deviant personality

6

Possible answers
public opinion
usual formula
odd idea
unconventional behaviour
bizarre characteristic
received wisdom
conventional theory
peculiar personality

Reading passage 10

Questions 1–5

1

1 C   2 E   3 E   4 B   5 D

Questions 6–11

6 life cycle
7 developmental paths
8 social organism
9 aggression
10 risk
11 animal kingdom

Questions 12 and 13

12 B
13 C

2

Students' own answers.